Lo, the Former Egyptian!

Books by

LO, THE FORMER EGYPTIAN!

RHUBARB

LOST IN THE HORSE LATITUDES

LIFE IN A PUTTY KNIFE FACTORY

LOW MAN ON A TOTEM POLE

DESERT ISLAND DECAMERON
  (SELECTED BY H. ALLEN SMITH)

H. ALLEN SMITH *Lo,*

the Former

Egyptian!

LINE DRAWINGS BY LEO HERSHFIELD

DOUBLEDAY & COMPANY, INC., GARDEN CITY, N. Y., 1947

This volume is dedicated to my two children who, whenever I chide them for misdemeanor, grab up copies of my various books and wave them under my nose and cry: "YOU should talk!"

Note

People are forever asking me foolish questions about the titles of the foolish books I write. The title of this book, whether you consider it good or bad, was thought up by me and by nobody else. In the past I have written several books with "cute" titles and I have grown a little sick of them. I want to get away from cuteness because, among other things, it has been done to death; I am thinking of titles involving totem poles, eight balls, wounded tennis players, men on half-shells, putty knife factories, busts, and all that sort of studied fatuity. I have been told, however, that I should make the break gradually and that this book should have a title with a little silliness tangled up in it. I insisted that the title have some relation to the contents of the book; its meaning will become clear to any reader who struggles through Chapter One. As usual, though, I had to fight for it. One of the head editors of Doubleday & Company, which in turn is the biggest publishing house in the country, tried to sneak up on me and change it. He wanted to call this book: "My Mummy Was an Egyptian." I killed him.

Lo, the Former Egyptian!

Chapter 1

On that day in 1944 I was quietly minding my own business—a business in which I am growing old and gray in the service of myself. It was a day much like other days, devoted to frittering with wordage and waiting for the mail to come. Finding nothing more constructive to do, I got to thinking about the cometlike success I had achieved as an author, a success which has caused me to be lauded in newspapers from coast to coast as a vulgar, rude, boorish, nasty, vile, indecent twerp. And I got to thinking about what a pleasant place the world was before this book-writing bacillus made a moral leper out of me.

That was the world of Nineteen Hundred and Thirty-Nine. An extremely bum year when you consider September and the "counter-attack with pursuit" in Poland; but I was thinking of that part of 1939 prior to September, when every day brought pageants and parades in the Court of Peace at the New York World's Fair (soon to be jammed with long solid lines of vehicles of war) and when Their Majesties of Britain ate weenies on the lawn at Hyde Park. I went over to the shelf where I kept the files of *Time* magazine and found 1939 and by chance turned to the issue of May twenty-ninth and an article which began:

A man sitting quietly before his fire may be at peace, but he is not at rest. If he sits long enough:

1) He turns a gigantic somersault, once every 24 hours, because of the earth's daily rotation on its axis. If he lives half way between the North Pole and the Equator, this motion carries him along at some 700 miles per hour.

2) The earth's annual revolution around the sun swings him in an orbit nearly 200,000,000 miles across at a speed of 18 miles per second.

3) The movement of the whole solar system relative to neighbor stars takes him in the direction of Vega at about 12 miles per second.

4) The whole galaxy to which the sun and all other visible stars belong—the Milky Way—appears to be slowly rotating. Various regions in this great disk, six hundred thousand trillion miles across, rotate at different speeds. Mr. Sit-by-the-Fire swings around the centre of the Milky Way at 170 miles per second.

I read it, and had an impulse to scream, to holler for help, to yell: "Stop it! Let me outa here!"

For a little while I had a feeling that I should never again know complete rest and contentment—an awful thought when you consider that the motto of my family should be *Dolce Far Niente*, which is Italian for "sweet doing-nothing" or "sweet idleness."

(Now why did I have to say that? Why did I have to drag in that Italian phrase? I know why, and so do you. I hauled it in to show off. It's a thing that authors do, believing their readers will admire them for it, and now I catch myself doing it, reaching into the trash barrel of my mind and fishing out a fancy foreign phrase, and then going to the dictionary and checking to make sure I have it right, proving that I had no right to use it in the first place and that I could and should have said that there was a tendency toward laziness in my family. What hams most authors are! What a horrible ham am I! Dolce far niente my hind leg!)

So there I sat, going 700 miles per hour in one direction and 18 miles a second in another, and shooting 720 miles per minute in the direction of Vega and ripping around the Milky Way at a speed of 170 miles a second. I felt uncomfortable, and held my head while I thought about it, and I could almost hear an awful whistling in my ears. I got up and peeped out the window, but everything outdoors seemed to be in order, and some girls were playing tennis across the way, apparently unaware of the frightful pace they were setting, or being set.

Thus I was in no condition to withstand even a minor shock; but I got a major one when the postman came. There were two letters from southern Illinois. One was from a lady who used to dangle me, like a wet participle, when I was an infant physically. She enclosed a clipping, and when I glanced at it I saw my name and after it the identifying phrase, "a former Egyptian." The thing didn't coagulate at first. I mumbled "former Egyptian" a few times, struck or stricken by the impossibility of there being such a thing. I personally have never been in Egypt and know almost nothing about the place, yet this newspaper or magazine or whatever it was had called me a former Egyptian. How could anybody be a *former* Egyptian? Once an Egyptian always an Egyptian.

Then I caught on. I turned the clipping over and found it had been taken from a publication called *Egyptian Key* and that the slogan of the *Egyptian Key* was "Opens the Doors of Southern Illinois."

If you take a map of Illinois and draw a line east and west from Vincennes, Indiana, to St. Louis, Missouri, all that part of the state to the south of the line, with the Wabash River on the east, the Ohio on the south, and the Mississippi on the west, is called Egypt or, sometimes, Little Egypt.

I was born in the north-central part of Egypt and spent my first six years there. Thus it was altogether true that I am a former Egyptian. I read the clipping. It was a review of one of my books. A glow came over me, for here, at last, was recognition at home for the little Egyptian who went out into the world and made his mark. This is what I read:

. . . Filled with coarse comments and low stories of the near great, we are unable to decide whether he writes for the financial remuneration or whether he is a new form of Crusader. He may have the idea that his books will awaken the American people to a realization of the depths of good taste and morality to which we have sunk.

If the readers of his books will take to heart the lessons that can be deduced therefrom, they will become aroused to the need of a restoration of the American character. Our personal feeling in the matter is that Smith writes the type of rot that he does because he knows a certain large class of present-day Americans will buy it, thereby earning him royalties. The latest in this category of low-brow, coarse, crude reminiscences is published by Doubleday.

Hot damn! Honor in my own country! I fought down the impulse to rush right out and buy a beautiful silver loving cup and send it, in token of my appreciation, to the editor of the *Egyptian Key*. Full of low-brow, coarse, crude croton oil. I do not know the editor, but this I know about him: he is an abrupt movement, or jerk.

It was the second letter from Egypt that really shocked and confused me so that for a while I didn't care if I were traveling twelve hundred miles a second in sixty directions. This letter was from Veronica Hassett, a cousin of mine who lives in McLeansboro, Illinois—the town of my nativity. Before I relate what Veronica had written to me, I must lay a foundation.

Up to the moment that letter came I believed myself to be Harry Allen Smith, a native white American, born on December 19, 1907, in McLeansboro, Hamilton County, Illinois. I had no birth certificate attesting these facts, though I did have an affidavit signed by my father and mother.

Some time earlier Veronica Hassett had written to tell me that she had been able to get a birth certificate for my sister and did I want one for myself. During that wartime period, you may recall, thousands of individuals all over the country were engaged in a scramble for birth records. You may also recall from your own experience or the experience of your relatives and friends that American history had apparently missed the wholesale burning down of courthouses and city halls. I knew dozens of persons who had gone after their birth certificates and every one of them reported that the courthouse had burned down, or the city hall, or the church where they were baptized, or the grade schools they attended. It was my own understanding, in fact, that there was no possibility of my getting a birth certificate because the courthouse in McLeansboro had burned down, and also the church where I was baptized.

I was a trifle skeptical, but I told Veronica to go ahead and get me a birth certificate if she could. Now came her answer.

"It seems," she wrote, "that there is a lot of confusion about your birth. I have been going over the records in the clerk's office and I've found out that you were registered as Henry Arthur Smith and it looks very much as if you were born in 1906 and not 1907."

Jeezley!

Fortunately I was sitting down when I read it. A year added to my age in a fraction of a second! It felt like ten. And I was *not* Harry Allen Smith. I was not H. Allen Smith. I was Henry! I was Arthur!

Normally I get nervous and panicky over the most trivial crises. But *this* thing! Having my identity wiped out, and a long, solid year slammed down on my frail shoulders! I almost got hysterical. All sorts of alarming notions raced through my mind. I started to yell for my wife and then clamped my mouth shut. Lord! I wasn't even married to her! And my children—what did it make of them? I mean other than a loose, popular usage of the same expression.

There had never been a hint that anything was wrong with either my name or my age. I tried to find solace in the theory that my cousin had confused me with another Smith. There are such things—other Smiths. That a Henry Arthur Smith actually *was* born in McLeansboro the year before I, Harry Allen Smith, greeted the sunrise. No. It couldn't be. My father's name was and is Henry Arthur Smith. *He* wasn't the one born in 1906. It almost had to be his son, it had to be me.

In those moments I needed sympathy, the cool caress of a friendly hand, and so I called in the one person who has stood by me for twenty years, fighting the good fight at my right hand, understanding me and my ways, a source of lofty inspiration at all times. I told her the story and she studied the thing over a bit and then started laughing.

"Well," she said, "that's a good one! Always letting on that you're so young! Getting that crew cut so you'll look like a college boy! Now maybe you'll begin acting your age. Why," she said, "you don't even know who you are!"

"Don't try to be comical," I said. "This is serious!"

"Okay, Henry," she said. "Okay, Hank."

"Cut that out!"

"I'll have to admit," she went on, "that it'll be hard to get accustomed to living with a different man. That is, if the law allows it. Imagine me! Married to Li'l Arthur!"

I looked around for a blunt instrument but, finding none, allowed myself to cool off a bit. Then I asked her not to tell the children, not to tell the neighbors, not to say anything to the Streets. Then I myself went down to the Streets and got Jimmy into his study with the door closed and told him. He just sat there and laughed.

"You'd better call up Doubleday," he said, "and have them withdraw your books from the market, and destroy the plates, and give them back the money you've got out of them, and start all over again. That's an out-and-out fraud, pretending those books were written by H. Allen Smith."

"You," I said bitterly, "are a goddam unfeeling historical novelist. I came down here looking for sympathy, for a way out, and look what I get! A clown, yet!"

"Furthermore," he said, still laughing, "those contracts you have with Doubleday are now null and void. Under the law, they won't have to pay you a cent. You, my friend, are in trouble."

I sputtered out a slighting remark about the clothes he wore and then stomped out of the place and went back to my own apartment and started writing frantic letters.

In time I got the thing straightened out. I learned that I actually was born on December 19, 1906. My parents decided to name me Harry Allen. My father's name was Henry Arthur but he was always called Harry so Harry was the name they wanted for me; and they wanted my middle name to be Allen, which was my mother's maiden name. If the information in this paragraph is not quite clear to you, read it over again, two or three hundred times. If it still isn't clear, skip over to the next chapter. If you don't want to do that, throw the book away—you ain't smart enough to read.

My parents selected the names they wanted for me but, I found out, they reckoned without my grandmother Smith. She was a woman with a stainless-steel will. She thought I should be named Henry Arthur Smith, the same as my father. There was a small argument about it and she let it appear that she had lost. But she had her way. The doctor who brought me into the world was her son-in-law (father to Veronica Hassett). Grandma Smith saw to it that Doc Hassett, in turning in the record of my birth, made the name Henry Arthur Smith. And a while later she came to the house and carried me over to St. Clement's Church and had me baptized the way she wanted me baptized. I have deep respect for my antecedents, but I hope that as she carried me home from that church I baptized *her* a little. Meanwhile my parents knew nothing whatever of her secret activities and they brought me up as Harry Allen Smith.

What could I do about it? I could go secretly to McLeansboro and burn down the courthouse and the church. But I chose to put Cousin Veronica to work. She consulted with the county clerk and with a local lawyer. She ascertained that in order to have a birth certificate I would need an affidavit from my mother; the record she had dug up was merely an entry in some sort of a ledger. On the basis of the affidavit the clerk would issue a certificate. I was notified that I could choose my own identity and age.

I chose to continue through life as myself. That is, as myself was, or had been, or thought I was all along, regardless of error. I had come along for thirty-odd years under one banner; I decided to stay under it. The certificate was issued to Harry Allen Smith.

As for my age, the certificate says I was born December 19, 1907. That makes me, at this writing, thirty-nine years

17

old. But I know damn well I'm forty. And I keep getting mixed up about it.

The most disturbing feature of the whole business is the fact that I can't seem to locate the lost year. I can't remember ever having skipped a birthday. It is inconceivable that the year was lost out of my infancy; parents simply do not make that kind of an error.

There remains the probability that I myself knocked a year off my age at one time or another. Most of my friends, knowing the quality of my mind, believe they have the answer. They say it is obvious that when I was young I was left back a year in school, and that I reduced my chronological age by one year in an effort to avoid the jeers of my classmates. This theory is completely scurrilous, the product of diseased minds.

When did I lose that year? In all honesty, I don't know. I can't remember.

A man who is unable to recall the loss of an entire year out of his life surely is the poorest candidate on earth to write a memoir of his childhood. That's one of several reasons why I'm doing it.

Chapter 2

The first book issued under my name, or the name I thought was my name, by my present publishers, had a blurb on the jacket—a blurb which suggested rather forcefully that the reader would find, inside that book, the greatest piece of writing in the history of the printed word. The blurb also described the volume as "a travel book by a man who has never gone anywhere."

That latter statement, I'm afraid, is a slight exaggeration —the only time exaggeration has ever been found in connection with any of my books.

It is true, however, that I have done little traveling in an age when almost everybody else worships The Wheel. Yet I come from a traipsin' family. My mother, my father, and all my brothers and sisters "take trips." My mother is heading in the direction of seventy, and as her years increase, so does her stamina. She enjoys nothing so much as riding halfway across the continent in a bus or sitting up for three days and three nights in a railway coach. She'll be at home reading her newspaper and she'll come upon an item reporting, say, that a new A & P store has just been opened in West Virginia or Utah or Saskatchewan. "Well, I declare," she'll say. "I think I'd like to see that." And in no time at all she's on a train or a bus, bound for a firsthand inspection of that new grocery store.

Apparently the genes got scrambled, for I inherited nothing in the way of a tendency to take trips. Whenever I do go on a journey the project becomes, in my mind, the greatest and most thrilling and most frightening adventure since the first flowering of Frank Buck. The thing has become a source of embarrassment to me. Suppose my business requires that I go out to Hollywood from New York. The date is decided and the train reservations at hand. I start telephoning everyone I know.

"Guess what!" I cry to my friends.

"You've gone on the wagon?" they usually respond.

"No! But that's close. I'm going on a train! Clean to California! Hollywood! On a train! And come back on one!"

The whole passionate tone of my announcement suggests that I expect my friends to chip in and get me a going-away present, something tasteful in solid silver, and that they should be at the station in a body with fife-and-drum corps at the hour of the great leave-taking.

At a time when millions of American boys were racing back and forth across the world, when motion-picture executives were commuting by plane between New York and Hollywood, I spent one solid week packing and unpacking and repacking two large traveling bags for an overnight trip from New York to Baltimore.

In other words, I have never been able to acquire a casual attitude toward travel. This condition dates back, I suppose, to my boyhood, when I lived in Midwest towns and when any sort of travel was looked upon as breath-taking. I remember, for example, an incident that took place when I was about fifteen or sixteen, nearing the age of reason. Another boy who had been a close friend had moved from Huntington to Fort Wayne, and I was invited to go to Fort Wayne and see a picture show and stay overnight at his house. I got two days off from my job as proofreader at the Huntington *Press*. I packed as if Mrs. Martin Johnson had asked me to come see her at her place of business. I was to travel the twenty-odd miles to Fort Wayne by interurban car. All members of my family who could possibly make it came to the station to see me off, and there were kisses all around, and also present were the managing editor, the city editor, the society editor, and three printers from the newspaper.

The interurban car came in Market Street from Peru and Wabash. Members of my bon-voyage party began shouting excitedly and slapping me on the back, and there were cries of "Take care of yourself!" And from the managing editor of my newspaper (who was a wit) such admonitions as, "Don't take any wooden nickels!" and "See you in the funny papers!"

I suppose all those people have changed, but I haven't.

This book, then, is mainly an account of some minor travels—minor by the standards of the day, but extremely major so far as I am concerned. Seven thousand miles! All over the dad-burned landscape! Drove every lick of it! Let Perleman have the great wide world—I'm satisfied with Egypt!

When I first came to New York in 1929 with moisture dribbling from the underside of my ears I looked upon Theodore Dreiser as many people look upon God. I could stand in the street outside his apartment and get the clammy-damps. I remember once being in an office building, two miles high, when someone remarked that Theodore Dreiser was visiting somebody in another part of the same building. I went weak all over. Me, in the same building with Theodore Dreiser! That big bum really sent me!

Please remember that I was quite young at the time and that we are all, I hear, subject to some form of imbecility of this nature when we are in the springtime of life. I was in my first childhood, and during that period any author of any book was immortal in my judgment.

Just before I left Denver for New York, Dr. Will Durant came to town for a lecture. I checked the hotels and got him located and went out and bought a copy of *The Story of Philosophy*, which was then a best seller. After that I telephoned Dr. Durant and made out that I was quite near to being the hottest newspaperman in Denver, and an admirer of his, and would he autograph his book for me. Without any great display of emotion he said he would and named the hour when I should call. I asked my city editor, Johnny Day, if I might do an interview with the famous man and Mr. Day gave me his famous dark look and said, "Listen, you idiot, don't you even know that Durant writes a column for the opposition?"

Dr. Durant was writing something when I got to his room and he didn't embrace me and kiss me on both cheeks when I walked in. Matter of fact, he was a bit frigid. He took my copy of his book without saying anything profound, without saying anything at all, and sat down and wrote at the top of the flyleaf, "Will Durant." I was right there, hanging over his shoulder, panting on his neck, and I uttered an impassioned protest: "OH! Please, Doctor! I wanted you should autograph it to me personally!" He sighed heavily and asked me my name and then under his own name wrote, "to H. Allen Smith. Denver. 2-6-28." Then he slammed the front cover shut and handed me the book, almost violently. His actions were saying for me to get the hell out of there, but I was too stuperous with glory to know it. Instead of getting the hell out of there I planted myself in a chair, assumed what I thought to be an air of philosophic curiosity, leaned forward just a bit, and said:

"Now. Tell me all about it."

Dr. Durant stared at me curiously for a moment, as if I had suddenly turned into an ill-disposed adder. Then he said:

"Young man, I'm busy. Please go."

I took the hint. The whole mortification of the thing didn't come down upon me until much later because I had my autographed book. It was long afterward that I looked back upon the incident and felt the horrible shame of it. O lost! O stone! O leaf! O unfound door! Where? When? Denver. 1928.

This author hunger of mine had sharpened, if anything, by the time I got to New York. No celebrity outside the literary set impressed me. I had an enviable job—that of writing a daily feature story for the United Press and of choosing my own subject each day. Once I read a note in the papers that Babe Ruth had become the proprietor of a hat store on Broadway and that there was to be a grand opening with the Babe attending in person. I telephoned Ruth's manager,

23

Christy Walsh, and said I wanted to write a story about the opening and what time should I be there. Mr. Walsh said I should come to his apartment on Riverside Drive at 7 P.M. and he would take me down to the hat store.

Mr. Walsh greeted me at the door. "We're just finishing dinner," he said. "How about some coffee before we start?" I said that would be fine, and he escorted me into the dining room. Some men were sitting around the table smoking cigars and drinking coffee and talking. Mr. Walsh introduced me around, and I remember that when he came to the Babe I was just slightly impressed; I didn't even hear the names of the others. I sat down and had coffee and listened to the talk, which was small, and gradually things began to come into focus. A big quiet guy on my left said something to me, and when I turned and looked at him I recognized Lou Gehrig. A bit later I found that the plump little man on my right was Knute Rockne. Across the table was Walter Johnson, and next to him was Red Grange. All that was needed to complete the picture was Bobby Jones and Tilden and maybe Man o' War. We rode down later to the hat store in two cars behind a motorcycle escort—the one real thrill of the evening for me—and all I can recall of the trip was that Knute Rockne sat next to me and talked about the excellence of the knee-action principle embodied in the knees of the new Studebaker.

What a thing for a callow young man from the Midwest to stumble on! Ruth, Gehrig, Rockne, Johnson, and Grange! But my author worship was too dominant and these sports characters had little or no appeal for me. Dreiser—now that would have been different! If Dreiser had been in that crowd I'd have come away with damp underthings. It took fifteen years for me to get myself back in balance, but I made it; given my choice today of shaking hands with Eddie Stanky or playing eight games of Guggenheim with Edna Ferber, I'd take second base.

At the time of Dreiser's death much biographical stuff was written about him, and his latest book was published along about that time, and these circumstances led me to reading old critical pieces about him. Somewhere in one of these essays I came on the statement that *A Hoosier Holiday* contained some of his best writing. It took me a long time to find a copy of that book, but at last I got it and read it.

It is a big fat book, published in 1916—an account of a trip which Dreiser took by automobile from New York to Indiana. The car was a 60-horsepower Pathfinder and belonged to Franklin Booth, an artist. Mr. Booth went along on the trip and did the illustrations for the book. The car was driven by a chauffeur, a young man cleverly named "Speed."

Dreiser was born in Terre Haute and lived there until he was seven years old, lived in four different houses during those first seven years. The family moved to Sullivan, Indiana, and lived there three years, then moved to Evansville for a year, and finally to Warsaw in northern Indiana. Theodore himself left Warsaw when he was sixteen and, except for a year at the state university when he was eighteen, had never been back to Indiana. Now he was going back and it was a Great Adventure, not alone for the fact that motoring such a distance was a novelty in 1915 but for the opportunities it gave him to sentimentalize his rude beginnings. He was going to return to the scenes of his childhood, and he started sighing and groaning and all but weeping about it in the very first chapter of his book.

I found *A Hoosier Holiday* a tough book to read because I was unable to get into the spirit of the thing; the sentimental maundering either gave me the willies or caused me to laugh at the wrong moments. Dreiser wrote descriptively of his journey, to be sure, but frequently he'd interrupt himself to heave a heavy thought, such as, "But what is one to say of nature?" Could this, I wondered, be the same man who once caused my tissues to twitch?

Quite early in the trip the Dreiser party stopped for a picnic lunch beside an abandoned canal in New Jersey. Speed, the chauffeur, made comic remarks. It wasn't so much what he said, but the way he said it. Beside the canal these three men discovered that the hard-boiled eggs they had bought in Paterson were spoiled, and there was much jocular byplay about that. Later they threw their empty beer bottles into the canal and began trying to sink them by

throwing stones at them. Dreiser reported that he alone
threw a hundred stones at the beer bottles. Then:

Finally we climbed into our car and sped onward, new joys
always glimmering in the distance.

"Just to think," I said to myself, "there are to be two whole
weeks of this in this glorious August weather. What lovely things
we shall see!"

I judged from this passage that every time, in the future,
they came to a stream or river or abandoned canal, they
would launch some beer bottles and throw rocks at them,

and I almost quit the Dreiser narrative before it ever got out of New Jersey.

Since this book influenced me to undertake an expedition of my own, there are a few more things I'd like to report concerning it. I noticed, for example, that Dreiser used the adjective "gauche" over and over again in describing people he encountered along the way. I don't mind the word, but he used it too often, as though he had just learned it. You shouldn't had oughta use nothing like that only once, and sometimes once is too often in the case of some words. I myself had occasion one day to use the word "jejeune" in a book and I've always regretted it.

Dreiser was socialistic in his thinking as early as 1915, and his travel book contains many a gripe against The System, many a protest against the injustices committed against poor people by rich people, and how nice the poor people are and how nasty the rich. I agree with him. I am on the side of the poor people until a perverse notion enters my head and I begin wondering what would happen if the caste were reversed—if the poor people became the rich people and vice versa. Somewhere I've read a nice line: Rich people are nothing but poor people who have money. If, as I said, the caste were reversed and the poor people became the rich people, how would the poor people behave? What is one to say of nature? Which way did they go? Whose deal?

One other bit about the Dreiser book: in the town of Defiance, Ohio, he stopped to get a shave. I decided to do the same.

Anyone with the perception of a retarded hog should be able to see how a book written by Theodore Dreiser back in 1915 set me to ruminating of my own boyhood in the Midwest and brought on a yearning to go back and look at things and feel sad about them. That's what Dreiser did. He journeyed from town to town where his family had lived, and he went to each of the many houses they had inhabited. He stood in the front of these houses and immense feelings surged in his breast. He'd go to a house where he had lived briefly as a child and he'd ask the people if he might enter and see the room which had been his bedroom. Once in that room, the sentiment would roll out of him in great lugubrious gobs. Now and then he'd come upon some old geezer who had known his father, and when that happened the effect on Theodore was similar to the effect created by a sharp blow on the head from a croquet mallet.

I figured a thing like that ought to be fun; it would do a fellow good to go back to the scenes of his childhood and groan. My own childhood was similar to the childhood of Dreiser. My family moved from one town to another and, in each town, from one house to another. That was the beauty part of it for both Dreiser and me. Most people, I suppose, setting out on such a sentimental journey would have but a single house in a single town to visit, and they'd have to cram all their sadness into one big dramatic performance. Dreiser and I . . . hell, we had dozens of places to go and mourn for the dear dead days of long ago and far away.

The late O. O. McIntyre preached fervently against this sort of adventure and never returned to his own home town in Ohio, arguing that such a visit would only bring disillusionment. He preferred to remember Gallipolis as it was. He was a nice man, this McIntyre, and I recall a couple of admirable things about him. For one thing, he liked Joan Crawford. And for another, he once wrote an immortal phrase. He got a letter from an advertising agency asking that he write a few words for them—"something that has never been written before in all history." He did it. He wrote: "Hoot nanny on the hickey." I couldn't go along with him, though, in his belief that one should never return to the scenes of one's childhood.

In spite of the fact that I left my home in Indiana when I was in my middle teens, I'm Midwestern to the core. My manner of speech gives me away every time, though some people on hearing me talk ask me what part of the South I come from. Not long ago I went into a pharmacy in Chappaqua, New York, to buy a pair of garters or a new plow handle or a chiropractor's license or some such thing. Whatever it was I bought, I said to the pharmacist: "Put it in a sack for me." He studied me for a moment, then said, "You're from the Middle West." He said that he is always able to spot a Midwesterner that way. An Easterner would say, "Put it in a bag for me." I didn't tell him why it is we say "sack" instead of "bag." The explanation may be found in Mr. Mencken's *Supplement I of the American Language*. A paper bag in the Midwest has always been called a "sack" because the word "bag" means something anatomical out there.

I still hadn't quite made up my mind to do a Dreiser when out came a book called *Midwest at Noon*. It was the work of an Englishman named Graham Hutton, and the moment I heard of it I began to burn. I considered it an outrage that a bloody Englishman should come in and write a whole dern book about my native heath. I was brooding about it when along came another copy of *Egyptian Key*.

Love that periodical! This time it was a review of a novel written by the former Egyptian from McLeansboro. The reviewer said my novel was "overrun with obscene language, lurid details, and sex." The book, according to the critic, "reeks with poor taste, sarcasm, and vulgarity." There was much more in the same vein, and after I had read it I sat for a while, silently bestowing my fondest blessings on the staff of the *Egyptian Key*.

Then, in the same issue, I came on a review of *Midwest at Noon*. If the *Key* had given me a going over, it had merely been a warm-up for Mr. Hutton, the Englishman. They hit him with everything but the office rat. Immediately I went out and bought his book and read it. I found that Mr. Hutton knows considerably more about the Midwest than anybody who works for the *Egyptian Key*, ever wrote for it, or ever read it.

Mr. Hutton's book is a serious, sociological study of the Midwest, and the region comprising southern Illinois, or Egypt, doesn't quite appear in its pages as a modern Utopia; nor do the Egyptians themselves shape up as the most progressive and cultured people of the Western Hemisphere.

I suppose it is natural for the *Egyptian Key* people to be belligerently proud and defensive about their homeland. It seems altogether correct for them to defend Egypt against all contumely. Especially if a furriner, an Englishman, utters the fancied slurs. The *Key* reacted savagely just as I reacted savagely when I first heard of the book. I couldn't imagine how an Englishman would possibly be able to understand the most basic things about the Midwest.

An Englishman, I figured, wouldn't even be able to understand the language of the people. From the time of Ruggles and even before, the Englishman's inability to comprehend American talk and customs has served as a source of great merriment for Americans. During the recent war I remember a story about an English editor who was working on some copy handed in by an American writer. He came upon the phrase, "So's your old man." He changed it to, "Your father is also." Almost as bad as the French. You'll remember the celebrated response given by Brigadier General Anthony McAuliffe to a German ultimatum. General McAuliffe said, "Nuts!" The French newspapers were praiseful, of course, but the general's expression had them confused. They finally translated it: *"Vous n'êtes que de vieilles noix."* In other words, "You are nothing but old nuts."

Yes, I could understand the little magazine's indignation over Mr. Hutton's book. Only one thing could be worse, from the *Egyptian Key's* point of view: that would be for *me* to write a book about the Midwest and about Egypt.

Let us proceed.

Chapter 3

My wife went along with me on the trip. My daughter refused to go, there being no radio in the car.

But let's not start quite yet. Let's divagate some more. It's expected of me. Last year the *New Yorker* referred to me as the leader of a school of writing. The *New Yorker* didn't put it exactly that way; the magazine called me a *chef d'école*, the theory being, I suppose, that most of the *New Yorker's* readers are French. I've lost the clipping and I've spent two hours trying to find it without success. I imagine the girl cat ate it; she's been doing cart wheels and back flips on the front lawn lately. I can't quote it exactly, but I remember that the critic said the members of the *école* of which I am chef simply sit down at their typewriters and let the typewriters run away with themselves.

Insofar as I, the chef, am concerned, it is true. My typewriter has a definite tendency to get out of control. If there were any organization to my craftsmanshiplessness, we should by now be on our way to Egypt. We should, by this time, be somewhere west of Elmira. But my typewriter has the urge to deviate, to tell a story about my daughter who didn't go with us and whose name is Nancy.

One day I was in conversation with George Jean Nathan. We were talking about a man who believes that the loser in our presidential elections should be, on the day after election, taken out and hanged for the obvious reason that otherwise he's going to be around getting in everybody's hair. I have reference to H. L. Mencken.

Mr. Nathan said that Mr. Mencken was unique among men "because he had an altogether happy childhood." Mr. Nathan is of the *école* which believes that childhood is a time of tragedy and not happiness. One of the things he had in mind is the fact that children are cruel little brats. In their relations with one another, children are the most cruel animals on earth next to adults. I know this because I am a parent; I know it from observing my own and others, and it so happens, as I've suggested elsewhere, that at one time I myself was a child and remember parts of it, both give and take.

Recognizing the cruelty of one child toward another and the general unhappiness of juveniles, I have refrained, up to now, from writing much of anything about my own children. Now they are all but grown, and they can counterpunch pretty well and know the uses of insult and are thus prepared for social intercourse on an adult plane. I can write about them and they will not be wounded any more severely than other people about whom I write, including the editorial staff of the *Egyptian Key*. In proof of the fact that they are grown I advance the evidence of my son. When he was about thirteen years old a book of mine was published and had some success, and soon thereafter I went to work at writing another, being greedy for money. He and his sister came to me one day and said they had a serious matter to discuss with me.

"Is it true," asked my son, "that you are writing another book?"

"Yes."

"Well," he said, assuming the manner of a shop steward, "we wanted to ask you a big favor. In the next book please don't put any swear words in it."

I whipped them and cut off their allowances for two weeks and ruled out movies for a month.

In 1946, when this same son of mine had reached the age of eighteen, he came home from college, criticized my haircut, cleaned out petty cash to buy jump records, drank a bottle of beer, and then went for a walk with me.

"I hear," he said, "that you're writing another book."

"That's right."

"How's it going?"

"Well, it's almost finished."

"Is it any good?"

"Certainly it's good. What kind of education you getting up there, anyway?"

He lit a cigarette off another cigarette.

"Have you got plenty of sex in it?" he wanted to know.

"Well," I said hesitantly, "well . . . quite a bit."

"That's the stuff!" he said with enthusiasm. "Put plenty of sex in 'em! That's the stuff they want!"

I was secretly outraged and was very careful not to take his corrupt advice, but his attitude convinced me that he was no longer a little boy, and that his sister was a big girl now, and that I might feel free to write about some of those things I've been hoarding for so long.

So it is that my vagrant typewriter and I choose, at this point, to tell a story concerned with the Sinatra daffiness. Frank Sinatra is still around, still doing well for himself and punching the right people, but much of the hysteria has waned and it is possible nowadays for him to appear in public with a good chance that he won't have his suspenders jerked off by his juvenile admirers.

The world knows how the Sinatra Plague swept the United States and possessions a few years ago, seizing as its victims those girls who were on the very doorstep of womanhood, addling the contents of their brainpans and confusing their tongues. To my knowledge I am the only parent among hundreds of thousands who whipped the thing without recourse to chloroform or a baseball bat.

The disease hit my house when my daughter was fourteen; she and her little group of girl friends took down with the murrain and stayed semiconscious for months. When Frankie's voice came over the radio other members of the family were not permitted to speak, whisper, or use the sign language; no one was allowed to move around, scratch himself, or belch.

I made the error once of uttering a disparaging remark about Mr. Sinatra. I didn't say I thought he looked like an ailing toad-frog. I simply remarked that I didn't think he was particularly handsome. Five girls, including my daughter, quit speaking to me for three weeks. I regained my standing only through an abject confession of ignorant error.

When Sinatra-time arrived those girls would issue their demand for sepulchral silence ten minutes before The Voice arrived in the room. They'd sit and listen and pretend to swoon with each bar of music, as was the fashion. When he did little tricks with his larynx they'd drop back into their chairs, roll their eyes up corpse-fashion, and go limp.

The walls of their rooms were converted into fantastic galleries. They clipped every interview, feature story, gossip item, and picture of their hero from newspapers and magazines, and these they glued to the walls. One of the girls had a blowup of his head fastened to the ceiling directly over her bed so that he would be gazing down at her when she awoke each morning.

Their conversations were of nothing else, and the telephone talk was both marvelous and maddening. "He" and "Him" meant but one person. In the midst of this pestilence circumstances arose which, in the end, gave me an opportunity to rid my house of the bug. I moved to Hollywood, having been engaged to stare at walls for Paramount. I put my daughter in school at Azusa and she was permitted to come in to Hollywood for occasional week ends.

Sinatra had just recently become a resident of Hollywood. I had never seen one of his broadcasts but I had heard that they were screwy affairs, so I arranged to risk life and limb by attending one at the CBS Playhouse on Vine Street. A few days before the broadcast I met Marc Connelly and he told me he was working on a motion-picture story based on the Sinatra legend. Mr. Connelly mentioned the fact that he had never seen Sinatra, nor had he ever heard the guy sing. I asked him to go along with me to the broadcast.

We arrived at the theater early in the afternoon to find the germ carriers lined up out front. They were in double file and the line stretched two blocks down the street. We talked to some of these girls and found that most of them had been on the line since eight o'clock that morning, though

they wouldn't be admitted to the theater until fifteen minutes before six in the evening. Among them we found a group of Chinese bobby-sockers. They called themselves "The Five" and they were dedicated to the uninhibited worship of Frankie. They told us that they had bought a present for their Frankie that very day. It was a handkerchief and it had already been sent in to him. They enclosed a note with it which said:

"Please, Frankie, wear this handkerchief in your coat pocket for us today. But after today we don't want you to wear it in your pocket. We want you to *blow your nose on it.*"*

Mr. Connelly and I went into the empty theater and took seats for the rehearsal, during which Mr. Connelly had opportunity to observe the singer in action. Then we adjourned to the Brown Derby to talk it over, returning to the theater as time for the broadcast drew near. We took seats on the front row where it would be convenient for us to turn around and watch the faces of the audience.

They didn't open the front doors and keep them open. They let the afflicted girls enter in waves—about thirty to a wave. That in itself was a spectacle worth seeing. There we sat, alone in the quiet auditorium. A burst of shrieks signaled the entrance of the first demented wave, and wave is the word. Half of the girls in that first wave scorned use of the aisles and came right down the center of the auditorium. It was the only time in my life that I have ever seen people run at full speed across the tops of theater seats. The race was for the first row and not a girl was killed or maimed. In a moment Mr. Connelly and I were surrounded by babbling, chattering, excited sub-females. Most of them carried autograph books and a couple grabbed Mr. Connelly.

"Are you connected with him?" they demanded.

"With whom?" asked Mr. Connelly.

"Frankie!" they cried. "Who else?"

"No, I'm sorry," said Mr. Connelly. "We are just spectators."

That was all the attention we got. Had we been connected in some way with Frankie, had we been clients, say, of the same advertising agency which had Frankie's sponsor for a client, then we'd have been important and our names would have gone into the autograph books.

The curtain went up about five minutes to six, and somebody introduced the band leader and then Frankie came on-stage. The girls screeched like passengers on an exploding

The italics are Max Shulman's.

36

steamboat and Frankie turned his face toward them. He smiled, ever so wistfully. They shrieked three times as vigorously. All during the show that guy had only to glance out at the audience to send those girls into spasms. The kids in the front row fastened their chins over the lip of the stage, fastened their eyes on Frankie and never once took them off. Sledge hammers couldn't have moved them.

We sat through the broadcast, listened to the squeals and whinnies, and when it was over we started out by way of the stage entrance. Backstage I saw Sinatra in a corner writing with a pen and with him was George Evans, his press agent. I knew Evans from New York and went over and asked him, in a moment of weakness, if I could get an autographed picture for my daughter. The Voice obliged and I mailed the thing out to school.

I should have known better. That picture sent her temperature to a new high, aggravating the miasma to a point where its chief symptoms were loss of appetite and chronic trance.

Something had to be done about it.

I was having my shoes shined on the Paramount lot one afternoon when George Brown came along with a couple of ladies and introduced them. I was interested in one of them more than the other, for she was Sue Carol, wife of Alan Ladd. I knew that Alan Ladd was the Number Two man in the affections of my daughter and all her friends. He had been top man before Frankie came along and he was still up there close in second place. I explained this state of affairs to Mrs. Ladd and made a proposition which she accepted.

The following week end Nancy came in from Azusa, and on Saturday morning I took her on a tour of the Paramount studio. She met a number of picture stars and was reasonably impressed, and grateful to me, and we went home early in the afternoon. Then I told her that I had to make a business call on a producer and she could go along. She said she was tired and that she didn't care particularly about meeting any producers but that if I wanted her to go, she would go. She asked me the name of the producer we were going to meet and I couldn't think of anything to say except Sistrom.

We drove out Los Feliz Boulevard and up Rufus Blair's

street and stopped in front of a house. As we went up the sidewalk I saw Sue Carol open the front door. I took a few steps ahead, winked at Mrs. Ladd, and said loudly, "Mrs. Sistrom, this is Nancy."

"Mrs. Sistrom" welcomed us and led us into the living room where we stood talking for a minute or two.

Then into the room came this guy. He had on nothing but a pair of sneakers and swimming trunks. Nancy turned around and looked at him and grabbed her face with her hands and started making noises in her throat as though she had swallowed fifteen cents' worth of bubble gum.

I led her over to a chair and eased her into it. She hadn't taken her eyes off Mr. Ladd. It turned out that he is a shy sort of person, that he was almost as embarrassed as Nancy, that he didn't know what to say, what to talk about. He got into a chair opposite Nancy, keeping his eyes averted from her, and finally said, "Let's have a drink." I asked Nancy what she would like to have and she gurgled unintelligibly and I ordered a coke for her. Mrs. Ladd went to get the drinks.

We sat there in silence for a while, then Mr. Ladd and I started talking about motion pictures and the Army. Occasionally he would steal a glance at the cataleptic creature opposite him, then quickly look away. Mrs. Ladd and the drinks arrived. Mr. Ladd picked a glass off the tray, stood up, walked over to Miss Smith, held it out, and said:

"Here you are, Nancy."

She took it with a trembling hand. She looked into his face and said:

"I've got friends back in New York who're just gonna *die* when they hear this!"

Mr. Ladd retreated to his chair. Mrs. Ladd went upstairs and got the baby and brought it down. Nancy asked if she might touch it. Permission granted. She touched it. She then managed to summon sufficient parts of speech to say that it was the sweetest, prettiest, loveliest, most beautiful, most gorgeous baby she had ever seen in her life.

At length we decided to go, and as we moved toward the door Mr. Ladd got up and said for us to wait a few minutes.

38

He went into the dining room, got a photograph of himself, and wrote something on it for Nancy—something about thanks for coming and to come back again soon.

I took her by the arm and led her back to the street, and driving home she sat with a blank look in her eyes. I took her up to the apartment. All she had to say to me, repeated over and over as though addressing God, was, "Oh, thank you! Thank you! Thank you!"

Her mother had to take her shopping, but it was an hour or so before her knees were steady enough for routine walking. She just sat and quoted the words he had spoken to her.

" 'Here you are, Nancy.' 'Here you are, Nancy.' That's what he said. To me. In person. Mother, he said, 'Here you are, Nancy.' He used my name. 'Here you are, Nancy.' In person! Oh, you don't realize what it means! You *can't* understand what has happened to me! Back home we always said the one thing we wanted to see most of all in this life was Alan Ladd stripped to the waist. And there he was! *In the flesh!* 'Here you are, Nancy.' 'Here you are, Nancy.' "

I thought of calling Dr. Harry Cagney and having him operate, but after a while she seemed to improve slightly. That evening a miracle bloomed—she *completely forgot* to tune in Frankie's radio program. She was gone, gone into another world. Her report card for the following month was a fright. Her letters contained nothing but Alan Ladd talk.

Something had to be done about it.

The next time she came in to Hollywood I took her again to Paramount. We went on the set of *Going My Way*. Bing was there, garbed in cassock and Roman collar, looking about twenty-five years old. He was off on the side lines talking to a couple of Waves. Before long he excused himself and came over and I introduced him to my daughter. He talked to her for half an hour. He sang a little song for her, something about a mule. He asked her about her school. He asked her what songs she liked and he sang another one for her. Then Leo McCarey called him back to work and he all but kissed her good-by.

She was stumbling when I got her away from that sound stage. She had locomotor ataxia with chills.

Outside I found a bench and settled her onto it.

"Oh!" she sighed. "Ohhh! Ohhhhhhhhh! Those blue eyes! And that Voice! Oh, thank you! Thank you! Thank you! Oh, Daddy, I love him!"

"What about Frankie?"

"Oh, pooh! Oh, Bing, Bing, Bing!"

"What about Alan Ladd?"

40

"Bing, Bing, Bing!" she repeated.

I had killed off Sinatra and in the process given her the Alan Ladd shakes. Now I had killed off Ladd and she had the Crosby trembles. But that was all right. Paw sorta goes for Crosby himself.

Chapter 4

For a time it looked as though I'd have to return to the scenes of joyous childhood in an automobile that was put together back in the days when there were five separate and distinct gleams in Mr. Oliva Dionne's eye.

This reverse exodus, into the land of Egypt, was undertaken at a period in our national economy when it was all but impossible to get a new car without going out behind the garage and slipping the dealer two and a quarter million dollars. I was at the top of the waiting list for a De Soto but there were no De Sotos. Then at the last minute Devoe Bingham, the Chappaqua dealer, came through with a Plymouth and we were ready for the wild green yonder.

Admiral Byrd didn't take much more equipment to Little America than we loaded into that Plymouth. I wanted to haul along a dozen empty beer bottles and a boxful of rocks to throw at them in case we came to an abandoned canal, but there wasn't room. Alert to all possible emergencies, we carried with us a tea towel in case we should happen to slobber some tea on ourselves.

In addition to several notebooks which I would use to set down the temper of the people, witty observations, descriptive passages, and overheard conversations, we carried a little book in which I carefully recorded the mileage reading at the beginning of the trip. At the first opportunity I had the gas tank filled and set down the amount of fuel taken on and the mileage at that moment and the cost. There was going to be system and organization to this expedition and when it was finished I'd have a complete record of every mile traveled and every gallon of gas burned and so on. Somewhere around Peekskill I put the little book in the glove compartment and forgot about it for the remainder of the trip.

Our first overnight stop was at Ithaca, New York, and Cornell University. Here we were guests of the fraternity to which my son belongs, he being a student of chemical engineering at Cornell. The fraternity house was an old mansion called "Llenroc," which is Cornell spelled backward. Ithaca spelled backward is Acahti. The mansion, Llenroc, took its name from its original owner, Ezra Cornell, inventor of the telegraph pole and founder of the university.

I had never been in a college fraternity house before and the whole experience was pleasurable because it afforded me an opportunity to witness my own son in the unbelievable act of behaving himself. Here was this roughneck kid of mine getting "A" in deportment all over the place. Everything at Llenroc was conducted on a genteel plane: the young gaffers put on ties and coats when they went in to dinner and comported themselves at all times as though they were junior members of the Union League Club. I did hear some vague talk about how one of the members had "flatfooted a pint" a couple of nights earlier. It was quite a while before I found out the meaning of the phrase. To flatfoot a pint is to stand with the feet flat on the floor, place a full pint to the lips, tilt back the head, and consume the entire pint without once moving the bottle. Sounds like professionalism to me.

After dinner at Llenroc coffee was served in the library, and these boys, including my son, stood around in little groups flatfooting demitasses and talking about international matters and the Administration, leisurely and unabashed and self-possessed. Personally I paid little attention to this talk, not being John Gunther. And then they sang in a way that made me think of the rangers in *Rio Rita*, sang about Cayuga's waters and Minnie the Moocher, and imagine my surprise to suddenly find myself hauling off and doing a little baritone job myself.

43

Such was my pleasure that I even overlooked the fact that my son had on my favorite necktie, which had disappeared from the house the previous autumn. And later on, when some of us sat around in the music room and engaged in polite conversation anent topics of the day, I couldn't help but think back on the scenes of *his* childhood.

He has a mathematical mind, a scientific bent, and has always excelled in such subjects as physics and solid geometry and hollow geometry and trichinosis, and this is a great mystery to his old man. In my own line, about three generations back, there was a Smith who could add without using his fingers, and among my wife's forebears, according to family tradition, there was an eccentric ancestor who could subtract. It baffles me that I should be the parent of a young man who understands things like bent space and atomic bombs and supersonics and radioactive isotopes and pituitary glands and mixing dry martinis.

The relationship between father and son, in our case, is a little on the strange side. Since he entered high school it has been a difficult matter for us to have any sensible conversation. In those early high-school days he used to come upon me quickly and say:

"What about Spinoza?"

"Well," I'd respond defensively, "what about him?"

"Give me a quick idea what he thought," he'd say.

For a while I tried to run a bluff, but it was no use. He had gotten out of hand, and as soon as Science captured him I gave up altogether. Now when he's home we sit at the dinner table and he rambles on about formulae and Nutrient X and how to create artificial snowstorms and where Albert Einstein slipped, and all I can do in the way of salvaging my self-respect is to interrupt with something like, "Got another royalty check today. Nice fat one."

Long ago he gave up asking me for the answer to anything, except that he sometimes solicits my opinion on whether the Brooklyn Dodgers will come out of their current slump. I suspect that he has nothing but contempt for writers and writing; just lately, however, he has become interested in reading short stories, but he finds things in them that I fail to see and we don't do so well conversationally on that score. I still raise the voice of parental authority and give him hell when he bangs up a fender of the car or sneaks my new set of golf clubs away from the house or takes on too many highballs; but I do it halfheartedly and in a spirit of resentment over the fact that he is quietly laughing at me because he knows so damn much more than I do.

I know a million stories about him, most of them being concerned with the intense, headlong manner in which he tackles Life. He seems to me to overdo everything he undertakes. Once when he was seven years old his mother took him on a train trip to Missouri. Being a human, she decided that she would pass him off as a mere infant and save the price of his transportation. She managed to get him into clothes which he had worn a couple of years earlier and then instructed him carefully in the art of pretending to be five years old. When the conductor came around to get the tickets this "five-year-old" was reading page one of the New York *Times*. The gangling kid in the clothes that didn't fit glanced up from his morning paper and cooed: "Is ooo duh tun-dutt-ter?" It was a moment of great embarrassment for his mother, who had it coming, but she stuck with her story and got away with it.

Soon after this my son took down with souvenir collecting. For about a year he had to have a souvenir of everything he did. He filled a couple of scrapbooks and two or three orange crates with junk. After a visit to his grandfather's farm in Missouri he glued into his scrapbooks such items as these:

"Lespedeza from feild. Dont tuch."
"Clover from clover feild. Dont tuch."
"Grass from front yard. Dont tuch."
"Grass from back yard. Dont tuch."
"Part of Hawker Hurricane. Dont tuch."

I don't know where he got his hands on part of a Hawker Hurricane but he had it, and he had one box filled with rocks—just plain rocks—which he had picked up in various localities.

I remember back when he was about ten and we lived on the ground floor of a house on Long Island. On this day I overheard a violent argument being conducted on the steps outside the front door. I couldn't make out the nature of the

45

issue involved, but before long my son came in and asked me for a nickel.

"What do you want a nickel for?"

"To make a bet," he said.

That was better. More reasonable.

"What's the bet?"

"Eddie," he said, referring to his friend from the apartment house across the street, "Eddie says he hit his grandmother with a blackjack last Tuesday and knocked her cold. I bet him a nickel he didn't."

"How are you going to prove it?" I asked, reaching for a nickel. I have sporting blood in my veins.

"We're going up and talk to his grandmother," he said.

"See if he'll go for a dime," I said. "I'll take half of it." And I gave him a dime.

After a while I heard more loud talk on the steps so I went to the door. My son, with characteristic devotion to his old man, had forgotten about my share in the wager. I called him inside.

"Well?" I said.

"We lost," he confessed. He explained that he and Eddie had gone up to Eddie's home and confronted Grandma.

"Did I or didn't I," Eddie asked her, "take a blackjack and hit you on the head with it last Tuesday and knock you cold?"

"His grandmother," reported my son, "said it was so, and she called him a bad name."

"Maybe she's in on the deal," I suggested. "Maybe she's taking a cut."

"I thought about that," he said, "so I told them I wanted proof. His grandmother showed me the bump on her head and then showed me the blackjack. It belongs to Eddie's mother."

I lost money on the transaction but I got a little contentment out of the knowledge that my own children had not yet started clouting their elders with blackjacks. I think I became a better father after that. My son didn't have to ask twice for a bicycle.

As he put on years certain peculiarities of his conduct became a source of irritation to me—such as his habit, when

46

he was around thirteen, of uttering high, sad whinnies at the dinner table. I tried to realize that he was a normal boy and that he had not taken to slugging his papa with blunt instruments, and I tried to be tolerant, knowing that some-day his little eccentricities would pass away, like milk teeth.

He went to a movie in which Robert Taylor played a prize fighter who carried a rubber ball in his hand and continually squeezed it to strengthen the hand. My son be-gan carrying such a ball and squeezing it. I advanced no objection to this except to make him put the damn ball down at mealtimes. Then came Dynamic Tension. I well remem-ber the evening when I first became conscious of its arrival.

The boy went through a session of the fidgets, tried to stand on his head, and then spent about twenty minutes saying, "Urk, urk, urk, urk, urk." After a time he eased up on the animal noises and, strange to relate, kept absolutely quiet for a long time.

From that moment forward his behavior pattern changed. He began doing things with chairs, dragging them around the house and performing wrestling operations on them. Then he announced that he wanted to go to the Bronx Zoo. This seemed an unusual yearning to come upon him during school term and in the dead of winter. Why did he want to go to the zoo?

"To see a lion," he said.

"But you've seen a lion," I argued. "You've seen plenty of lions."

"Yeh," he admitted, "but I never noticed it before."

"You mean you saw a lion and didn't *notice* the lion?"

"No," he said. "I mean I never noticed Dynamic Tension."

Then I knew the full, horrible truth. He had read a maga-zine article concerned with the doings of Charles Atlas, the man with the muscles and the leopard skin. Mr. Atlas teaches a thing called Dynamic Tension, which he learned off a lion. It consists, as Mr. Atlas puts it, in "pitting one muscle against another."

I realized that my son had been smitten by the muscle bug. The antics with the chairs stood explained. And I found out that he had made a secret trip to Macy's and come home with an iron dumbbell. He had been practicing with this implement in the privacy of his room, but now that his secret was out he brought it into the open.

He'd sit all evening, his homework spread in his lap and the dumbbell in one hand and the radio going. As he studied he'd raise the dumbbell above his head and bring it down and then thrust it out horizontally and fetch it back, and then go up again, and so on. It was distracting, but again I

put up with it. The thing that really drove me to despair was Dynamic Tension.

In pitting one muscle against another, Mr. Atlas had explained how he gets his arms and legs tangled up and fighting one another. He grabs his head and tries to pull it down with both hands, fighting back with his neck. He places the fist of one hand in the palm of the other and lets them battle it out to determine whether the fist can overpower the hand or the hand the fist.

My son had gone all out for Dynamic Tension, but the chief disturbing element lay in the fact that he refused to confine it to the house. I'd have been most happy if he had gone deep into some forest to pit his muscles against each other, but instead of that he'd come down our street practicing Dynamic Tension, letting his legs grapple with each other, fighting hands with fists, fists with hands, hands with neck, neck with hands. As these grotesque contests proceeded he'd groan and grunt with the effort. I was certain that the neighbors were watching these weird proceedings from behind their curtains. I was positive the neighbors were gossiping.

At last Dynamic Tension gave way to ballroom dancing. That boy decided he wanted to learn to dance expertly. He took money that might have gone for sodas or catcher's mitts and bought a book by Arthur Murray—a book whose pages were filled with footprints that might have been made by a drunk trying to get from the bar to the gents' room.

That was a trying period. He ruined the floors and defaced the sidewalks with chalk; he danced for hours, holding the book before him and using either a broom, a ball bat, or air for a partner when he couldn't get a human. One day I was called to the telephone. It was Arthur Murray's studio.

"Your son is here," said the lady, and I could tell that she was having a time trying to keep a straight face. "He says he wants to take our six-week course. But he says he doesn't want to waste six weeks on it. He says he wants to take the whole six-week course in three days. I don't know what to do about it."

I told her to shuffle him off to Buffalo and send him home. When he got home he had a set of drumsticks and a pad to beat them against and a booklet telling him how to do it. After that came eyesight. He found one of those books aimed at improving the sight through exercise of the eyes.

Cornelia Otis Skinner told me once how someone gave her a copy of such a book and she started reading it in the club car of a train carrying her from Hollywood to New York. She was sitting in the car reading about an eye exercise in which the forefinger is employed. She followed the instructions. She held up her right hand a couple of feet in front of her face with the palm turned outward and the index finger extended. The book said for her to move the finger from side to side, looking at it, then looking past it on one side, then at it again, then past it on the other side, keeping it moving back and forth all the while. She continued this exercise for a while and then she saw a man sitting beyond her finger. He was staring at her, almost leering. She yanked her finger down, realizing that to all appearances she had been sitting there wagging it at the man just as though she had been admonishing him, in a coy sort of way, as though she had been saying to him: "Ah, you gay dog! I know what's in your mind! Naughty, naughty, naughty!" Miss Skinner was so embarrassed that she scampered off to her bedroom and remained there the rest of the trip.

My offspring did the finger exercise along with a few hundred others. He hung charts around the house and filled his days with interminable chantings of the alphabet. He bounced things. There are no half measures with him. The book had been written by a prominent New York doctor, and one day the boy looked up the doctor's number and telephoned his secretary.

"It's about the doctor's book," he told her. "I bought it and paid good money for it. There are some things in it that are not quite clear to me, so I would like to have an appointment. I want him to explain them for me."

The girl told him that the doctor was a busy man and that she couldn't give him an appointment until sometime the following month.

"Well," he said, "never mind. I'm in a hurry."

There was nothing wrong with his eyesight and never had been anything wrong with it.

I was able to put up with Dynamic Tension, dancing with ball bats, and those eyeball exercises, but there came another obsession that almost sent me to an early grave. I didn't even suspect it until it burst upon me full-blown.

One evening a solemn gentleman from a big publishing house came to call. He and I were sitting in the living room when my son walked in. I introduced them.

The boy drew back the corners of his mouth to their maximum spread, giving him the appearance of a goat trying to remove shreds of ham that were caught in his back teeth. He bounded forward, seized the guest's hand, gave it a powerful shake, and then grasped the visitor's shoulder with his left hand.

"How are you, old boy!" he roared, losing much of the effect through the fact that his voice was changing. "How's Africa?"

"Africa?" repeated my guest, his voice faltering.

"Did you see the big-game country?" cried my offspring. "Thrilling! Tell me all about it!"

It was not overly warm in the room, and half an hour before he had appeared to be well and normal.

"Hey!" I interrupted. "What's got into you?"

He ignored me, still clinging to the man's hand, flashing that gargoyle grin.

"Tell me about yourself," he said. Then, without waiting for the guest to tell about himself, he plunged onward. "You have *beautiful* hair. Do you put anything on it? When's your birthday?"

This was a staggering piece of behavior when you consider that the boy had, up to then, been reserved in the presence of company, almost timid in meeting people. Something titanic had happened to him, and I found out what it was. That night I crept into his bedroom while he was asleep and found the answer on the table beside his bed. Again, a book. On the cover was:

THIS IS COPY NO. 1697576 OF
THE MOST POPULAR WORK OF NON-FICTION OF OUR TIME
HOW TO WIN FRIENDS AND INFLUENCE PEOPLE
BY DALE CARNEGIE

I came close to praying, close to falling on my knees and asking my Maker what I had done to deserve *this*. I resolved that I would wean him away from this thing or chloroform him and trust to the understanding of a jury. Surely they would look upon it as a mercy killing.

It took a bit of time and effort. He got so he would race to the telephone when it rang and sing out, in his changing voice, "Hello, there! Happy you called! Who is it, please?" He saved up his money until he was able to get a five-dollar bill so he might practice one of the Carnegie precepts. Whenever he found himself getting critical of someone, whenever

51

any problem of conduct presented itself, he would pull out the bill, look at the portrait on it, and say: "How would Lincoln have handled this problem?"

He went up and down the streets of the neighborhood collecting birth dates of people he scarcely knew, having resolved to send little notes of congratulation to them on their anniversaries.

I bought puzzles, games, other books, striving to get him away from No. 1697576. A basketball did the trick. I got him a full-sized basketball. He nailed up hoops in his bedroom and each evening had in Eddie, the boy who knocked his grandmother cold with his mother's blackjack. They played basketball by the hour, and the thumping and bumping and crashing was music to my ears and I never complained once about the wrecked furniture and the scarred plaster of the walls.

I don't remember what he did with his Lincoln bill, but on the evidence of his deportment that evening at Llenroc, I figure that he must have finally spent four dollars of it for Emily Post's book.

Chapter 5

At this juncture I want to salute a set of books—the American Guide Series. Anybody who travels without carrying along the guide for the particular states he is visiting is missing more than half the fun. A great many people know about these books but a great many more never heard of them. The idea for the series was born during the depression of the early thirties, and the individual books were put together by reporters and writers and editors in each state and in the major American cities under the authority of the Works Progress Administration. Whether I travel by car, by train, or by plane, I always lug them along. They are of exceptional value on automobile trips provided you have someone along who can read aloud as you go. Without them you miss most of the fascinations that clutter the open road.

If it hadn't been for one of the guides called *The Ocean Highway*, I would go to the grave without ever knowing that once in my life I crossed Stinking Gut Bridge. We were driving with the Matsons in North Carolina and I was doing the out-loud reading. We crossed Stinking Gut Bridge near Elizabeth City. There was no sign on it to identify it, but the book told us its name.

During that same trip we'd have driven past the Twin House without giving it a glance if the book hadn't tipped us off. The Twin House, or Twin Houses, is on the road out to Kitty Hawk, where Eli Whitney invented the hay tedder. One house, a two-story-and-a-half gabled residence, stands nearest the highway. Behind it, a bare ten feet away, stands an exact duplicate of the front house. The front house dates from about 1800 and originally was occupied by a husband and wife, typical Americans. What they fought about nobody knows. Maybe she used his razor to shave her legs; maybe she bought antiques; maybe she put sliced carrots in the pot of beans; maybe she was slow about shifting from first to second gear. Anyway, they quarreled bitterly, and I imagine the conversation went something like this:

"If you don't like it here, big boy, you know where the door is."

"Listen, sister, I built this house and no dopey dame is gonna put me out of it."

"Oh, forsooth, dry up! You know very well that this house is not big enough to hold us both."

"Well, then, haul your big fat can outa here and keep it out."

"Twenty-three skiddoo to you, Rhett! I happen to like this house. It was my idea, the way it's decorated, and who, pray tell, tatted the antimacassars?"

"Get this, you sluttish carrot-cooker-with-beans, I won't live in the same house with you another day—you lousy driver! I'll fix you! Where is the Head Slave? Gone to Elizabeth City to play the numbers, I'll vow! Wait'll I get my hands on that rascal!"

So saying, he stomped out of the house and located the Head Slave and together they staked off the back yard and before long they had erected another house exactly like the original. The wife moved into this house, where she could entertain her mother and other relatives to her heart's content, and husband and wife never spoke to each other again as long as they lived.

Stinking Gut Bridge and the Twin House are just two random samples of what you may find in the American Guide books as you roll along the highways anywhere in the land. On our trip West we carried the guides for the several states through which we would pass and my wife read from them as we went along. At Elmira, New York, my preliminary interest was chiefly in the town's association with Mark Twain and the fact that he is buried there. But the *New York State Guide* told me something that all but made me forget Youth Clemens.

The present name of the town was adopted in 1828. One of the early settlers, Nathan Teall, had a daughter named Elmira. Nathan also had a wife who possessed a voice that was shrill and penetrating and carried far distances. It seems that this girl Elmira was never around when her mama wanted her, and her mama was accustomed to yelling for her, calling her name from the front porch with such power and vigor that it was heard throughout the community. In 1828 the citizens grew dissatisfied with the town's name, Newtown, and decided to change it. The whole community apparently was Elmira-conscious from having heard Mrs. Teall bellow the name off her front porch, and so they made their choice. As I said, I virtually forgot about Mark Twain, and for the next couple of hundred miles the voice of Old Lady Teall rang in my ears, crying, "Ellll—myyyy—RUH!"

Every village, every town, and, to be sure, every city has its little stories, and most of them are set down in the guide books and if you don't have the guide books with you, you miss plenty. To jump ahead a bit, let us consider the town of Decatur, Indiana. It was of little interest to me that this was once the home of Gene Stratton Porter who wrote *The Girl of the Limberlost* (urp!). But it *was* of interest to have a look at the Auctioneering School operated by a Colonel Reppert in a building across the street from the courthouse. The school was not in session when we passed through Decatur, for which I was sorry because I'd have enjoyed watching the students at work. The school holds classes in July and December of each year. There are ten instructors and usually about fifty students. The students are first given a week of instruction in English, oratory, physical culture, psychology, and something called "pep." After that week of formal academic study they are sent out onto the street corners of Decatur for practical experience in auctioneering. The townspeople contribute the stuff which they sell and other townspeople buy it. I imagine it is a wondrous sight there in Decatur in July, with fledgling auctioneers whooping it up on every street corner, selling old dishes and busted chairs and discarded corset covers. I know I'd enjoy seeing and hearing it, and I think it would be pleasant, too, if during all that hullabaloo the shrill voice of Mrs. Nate Teall sounded over the rattling accents of the auctioneers, calling, "Ellll—myyyy—RUH!"

As we moved westward across Ohio it occurred to me that I was returing to the scenes of happy childhood in a somewhat bassackwards fashion. Childhood began for me in Illinois, continued for a while in Ohio, and ended in Indiana.

Defiance, Ohio, where I lived during the period when I was at my orneriest, is a town perched above the confluence of the Maumee and Auglaize rivers. It is about sixty miles southwest of Toledo and it was named by Mad Anthony Wayne who built a fort on the site and defied people. Later the site was occupied by troops under a tough officer named Winchester. This Winchester believed in discipline, and one day when a private was found asleep at his post he was sentenced to "ten cobs on his bare posterior, well laid on, with a paddle four inches wide and one half inch thick, bored full of holes." Thus it would seem that Defiance's contribution to civilization includes a form of punishment widely practiced by members of fraternal organizations, who band themselves together in a spirit of undying love and affection and whale each other across the bottoms with paddles much like the one described here. The "cobs" part confuses me a little. I think I'd better forget about it.

We came into Defiance from the south, and I didn't recognize a thing until we arrived at a parking place alongside the courthouse. I had deliberately passed up shaving myself that morning. Theodore Dreiser got a shave in Defiance; so would I. But I didn't. The first barbershop I entered contained one sad-looking barber and one customer, and the customer was in the final stages of a haircut. I walked in and sat down, and the barber looked at me over his glasses and said: "You got an appointment?" I said I hadn't. "Can't do nothin' for you," he said rather gruffly, "thout you got an appointment." I felt like telling him he could kiss my beast of burden, but I simply got up and walked out. I went to another shop. The barber told me I would have to get an appointment. I went to a third and got the same story.

Now at last an unutterable sadness came over me. Here I was, surrounded by the scenes of my childhood. Tender memories flooded in upon me. The boy had come back after a quarter of a century—that same boy who had gone from Ohio so many years ago without even a peach fuzz on his cheeks; and now he was back, his face dark with whiskers, and he had no appointment. This was the lovely and historic community where that boy had learned many things, including the finer points of cussing. Now, once again, he cussed—walked down the main street cussing the goddam jerk barbers and the goddam jerk town and kicking nastily at every curbstone he crossed.

Suddenly I found myself in front of a little movie theater, and the anger subsided and a fond recollection came back across the years. I remembered how it had been my custom to play hooky once a week for the purpose of seeing Eddie Polo serials. I stood outside for a while and recalled clearly that afternoon when I crept into the place and found a seat directly behind Old Man Hocker. There were only two or three other customers in the theater that afternoon, but it was a sure thing that Old Man Hocker would be there. He was a town character who apparently spent every afternoon of his life at the pitcher show.

On the screen that afternoon Eddie Polo was getting himself into a frightening dilemma. The villain had Eddie in a cabin, and I knew that the dirty dog was getting ready to wallop my hero good. He got some rope and lugged Eddie over to the cabin door and tied him to it—sort of spread-eagled him against the door. Then the big whiskered sheepherder picked up a blacksnake whip, let go with a few villainous laughs, and made ready to lay it on.

At this point Old Man Hocker turned around and hung his ancient chin over the back of his chair, facing the rear of the house, facing me.

"I ain't gonna look," he said. "I jist ain't gonna look. Not a bit. That dirty bastard ain't gonna hurt ole Eddie. I know it. I know it so well I ain't even gonna bother lookin' at it. I'm jist a-restin'."

"Turn around!" I yelled at him. "Eddie's gettin' loose!"

Old Man Hocker whipped his head back around to face the screen. Sure enough, Eddie Polo was down off that door. Wham! Down went the villain. In no time at all Eddie had *him* tied up to the door and *Eddie* had picked up the black-snake whip. It was just too beautiful for Old Man Hocker to bear. He stood up and waved his arms excitedly and hollered:

"Give it to 'im, Eddie! Give 'im some of his own medicine! Beat the son-of-a-bitch to death!"

I didn't go into the little theater, because I knew it would not be the same. For one thing, the people on that screen inside would be talking; and for another, I realized that the theater itself probably had been redecorated and refurnished half a dozen times since my time and the time of Eddie Polo. Furthermore, a certain hunger had come upon me—hunger for a banana split. I could remember that I always wanted to have a banana split upon emerging from the theater and that sometimes, maybe once a month, I'd get one. I turned around and scanned the street and there it was—the soda fountain where I had not only eaten banana splits but learned to construct them.

This was the real stuff of nostalgic yearning! A banana split would do the trick! All you have to do once you are back in the surroundings of boyhood is wander around and look at buildings and pretty soon things begin coming back. I entered the place and took a seat at the fountain. A young man and a girl were at work cleaning and polishing things and a small radio was going on the back bar and next to it I noted, with satisfaction, a plate containing three bananas.

In my day the architecture of a banana split was, as the saying goes, frozen music. When I took up jerking soda my boss spent at least an hour instructing me in the finer points of building this single heavenly dish. The split banana had to be placed just right in the boatlike dish. Then the three dippers of ice cream—called "scoops" nowadays but always "dippers" back yonder. After that came the chocolate,

plus an application of liquid marshmallow, and a couple of chunks of pineapple, and a cherry placed on the middle gob of ice cream. Over that a liberal sprinkling of crushed nuts. All done with extreme care under the eye of the customer, and no hurrying with it.

The girl slapped a paper napkin at me and said whadull-ut-be?

"I'd like to have a banana split," I said.

She looked at me a long while, rather resentfully.

"Did you say a banana split?"

"That's right."

Her attitude suggested that she'd like to split my skull.

Here was a girl who didn't enjoy her work. Remembering the pride with which we, in the old days, constructed a banana split, I got more than a little irritated.

"Look," I said, "you have some bananas over there in that dish. What're they for?"

"Cereal," she snapped at me.

"Well, I don't want any cereal. I want a banana split. Know how to make one?"

I was hoping she'd say she didn't, and that I could invite myself back of the fountain and build my own. But no, she knew how, and she went to work on it, and it was the sleaziest piece of work I've ever seen done. She simply threw it together, starting illogically with only *two* dippers of ice cream and ignoring the banana altogether. She squirted some sheep-dip and argyrol on the ice cream and then sprinkled coarse sawdust over the whole and then she got to the banana. Know what she did? She didn't split that banana. She *sliced* it. That dame was right out of a snake pit. She performed the entire operation in something like a minute and a half, and when she put it in front of me I sat and looked at it a long while.

It looked terrible, that 1946-model banana split, but I decided to try it anyway. Maybe it would taste all right in spite of the slovenly manner in which it had been put together. I was about to dig into it when the sounds coming from the radio hit my ear. It was a baseball game; not only a baseball game, but a baseball game involving the Brooklyn Dodgers. I don't know where it was being played—Cincinnati, probably. I do know that it did something strange to me. Here I sat in Defiance, Ohio, glaring at a jerry-built banana split, striving desperately to recapture one of the most pleasurable sensations of my youth—and Hugh Casey was pitching, and having trouble. In a flash I was back at Ebbets Field, hearing the shrill notes of The Whistler as he piped Whitey Kurowski back to the bench, and the thumpety-boom-bump of the Brooklyn Sym-phoney, and the Dodger-hater back of third base crying, "Here goes yer old balllll game!"

I put a quarter on the counter, got off the stool, and hurried away from that place. I wouldn't be surprised if they're still talking about it—the goofy-lookin' goon that come in that day and orders up, of all things, a banana split, and don't touch it but runs for the street like a black widder had bit him. I don't care. I don't care what they say. All I know is that anybody who would slice bananas onto a banana split—that person's grandmother sucks eggs.

So I moved on down the street and after a while came abreast of the bank where I had opened my first account and where I met my first bank president. At least I think he was a bank president. When I lived in Defiance I worked at odd jobs—built banana splits, delivered newspapers, clerked in a grocery and again in a shoe store, and during one period was a nailer in a box factory. One day I went to the bank and opened a savings account with a deposit of four dollars. It was a thrilling experience and remained thrilling until the next day, when it began to die down a little. I went to the bank and drew out two dollars of the four. After I had frivoled away one of the dollars, remorse set in and the following morning I redeposited the remaining dollar, giving me a new balance of three dollars. Two days later I drew out two dollars. The day after that I got paid at the shoe store, so I went back and deposited three dollars, fetching me up to my original holdings of four dollars. Then I let two whole days go by before I returned and drew out three dollars. This was the end. The teller told me to wait just a moment. He went backstage somewhere, and pretty soon I was called into an enclosure where sat the man I assumed to be president of the bank. He was straightforward, honest, and altogether aboveboard with me. He said:

"Young man, you have just withdrawn three dollars from our bank. You have a dollar balance. The teller is now withdrawing that dollar for you. I want you to take it and get the hell out of here and stay out."

My wife had gone to a beauty parlor to get her hair sorted out (it turned out that she got immediate service without an appointment), so I continued my wandering and finally I came to a landmark that brought a fresh flood of memory. Weisenburger's Rexall Drug Store. Many a long evening I loafed in Weisenburger's although it was not a hangout for kids. I loafed there for a reason: I was in love with Mr. Weisenburger's daughter, Helen. We were in the same class at St. Mary's Parochial School and I worshiped her, although she didn't know it. I've forgotten what grade we were in at the time we both switched from the main school building and enrolled for a business course which was taught in a little one-story frame house that stood between the church and the parish house. We studied shorthand and typing and bookkeeping and things like that. Helen Weisenburger was the star pupil of the school and the only pupil in the place who could put me down in a spelling bee. It was always an intense pleasure to me whenever Helen outspelled me, as I admired her no little.

In the business school we were required to keep a complete set of books for a mythical commercial establishment which, as I remember, dealt largely in oats, and I think that if it hadn't been for Helen Weisenburger's high scholarship I would have been drummed out of the joint before ever taking in my first imaginary peck of oats. Helen's bookkeeping was perfection, with trial balances balancing and debits and credits and accounts receivable and pay roll all in their proper places. Mine, on the other hand, was a botch and I always seemed to be far behind the rest of the class . . . until I discovered the unlocked window. It became a custom with me to go to the little frame building late at night, two or three times a week, raise the unlocked window, climb in, draw the shades, get Helen's books out of her desk, thrill to the touch of them for a while, cast off thoughts of love for the time being, and copy her figures into my own books with the aid of a small flashlight. O youth! O impetuous, cribbing youth! Ah, that I might go through those days of double entry once again! Nit!

I went into Weisenburger's. Helen's father was there, alone in the store, but when I introduced myself he couldn't seem to place me, so I didn't stay long. Instead I went back to the car, and soon we were driving around looking at different sections of the town. We crossed the river and rambled up one street and down another, but I couldn't seem to locate the first house the Smiths occupied in Defiance. Then we drove back toward St. Mary's church and school. I babbled in the manner of a Chinatown bus barker for the

62

edification of my helpmeet. I drove slowly along the street which I once traversed on foot en route to St. Mary's.

"Every morning," I said, "I'd come walking along this street, and every morning I'd meet the Miller brothers coming toward me, running at top speed, on their way to the public high school. Don Miller, you know."

"Who?"

"Don Miller. And his brother Jerry. For heaven's sake, doesn't the name Don Miller mean anything to you?"

"You couldn't mean that carpenter from Yorktown Heights?"

I lapsed into quiet disgust. No use to tell her that Don Miller went on from Defiance High School to become a member of Notre Dame's Four Horsemen, and to become one of my first heroes. No use to say that I was once on speaking terms with him. He and his brother, also a football player, used to start late deliberately each morning and run all the way to school. They'd come ripping down the sidewalk, and as they whipped past me they'd both yell out, "Hi!" And I'd yell out, "Hi!" That's how I was on speaking terms with one fourth of a famous backfield before it got famous.

There was no use of my sulking, so in a few minutes we were at St. Mary's. I wanted to take my wife into the church and show her the choir loft where I used to sing, where I even did "Adeste Fideles" as a solo one Christmastime.

"This trip," she said, "would be greatly improved if you'd quit lying so much."

So we drove to the other end of town, out near the Auglaize River, and I told about the time I tried to ice skate all the way to Toledo, and then I found the house where we had lived. It was a boxlike frame house painted an unmentionable brindle color. I didn't get out and stand in front of it and feel sad. I just parked the car and stared at it awhile and tried to think of something connected with it that would tug at my heartstrings. The only thing I could remember clearly at the moment was a small incident involving my brother Bill. In this house Bill spent one whole morning and part of an afternoon sitting moodily, brooding, getting up to pace the floor, and when my mother would ask him what on earth ailed him, he'd tell her to leave him alone, that he was wrestling with a problem. Finally in midafternoon he let out a triumphant cry.

"Got it!" he yelled. "Finally figured it out!"

My mother wanted to know what he had figured out. He said that he had been wondering where the word "pickaninny" had its origin. And finally he had puzzled out the answer. He said that a long time ago, down South, there was a Negro mammy who had a lazy child. One day she ordered this lazy child to get out of the house and get into the fields and pick some cotton. Whereupon the lazy child said: "No, mammy, I ain't pickin' inny."

That's all I could remember about the house and there didn't seem to be anything in it worth feeling sad about. I decided I wouldn't even speak of the pickaninny matter to my wife. I was about ready to drive away when my eye fell on a house across the street and a magnificent memory bellied up to me.

"My god!" I said. "There's where Mrs. Milligan lived. She's the one I threw the brickbat at. Ever tell you about that?"

"I'd rather not hear it," said my partner-for-life.

"But," I insisted, "it's kind of important. Old Lady Milligan caught me smoking a cigarette down by the river and told my folks and I got a licking for it. The next time I saw her she was sitting right smack on that front porch there, sitting in a porch swing. I got hold of this brickbat and let it go at her. Missed her. But the brickbat went through that big window there on the left, and Old Lady Milligan started screaming bloody murder and the whole neighborhood got into an uproar and she called the cops and——"

"I hope," interrupted my wife, "that you're not going to put *that* in a book!"

I had to just think about the rest of it. Pop didn't whip me that time. He decided on more drastic measures. He put an ad in the Defiance paper which said: "Wanted—place for Catholic boy, age 12, to work on farm during summer vacation." A few days after that a buggy pulled up in front of our house and out got a big rawboned farmer whose name, as I remember, was Heffner. Actually he was

not rawboned; how the hell can anybody be rawboned? But he was big, and when his buggy pulled away from the house I was sitting beside him. What followed was my first and last personal experience with the glories of farm life.

This Heffner had a farm as big as Idaho and no hired help. His wife did most of the chores while he worked in the fields. I don't ever want anybody to say that I never did a hard day's work in my life. That guy had me out of bed before daybreak, raced me through breakfast, and worked me steadily until sundown. Even then he wasn't satisfied. We'd come in and wash up and eat supper and then maybe the two of us would wander out into the yard. Mr. Heffner would glance upward.

"Be dog-gone!" he'd say. "Lookit that moon! Might near bright as day. Purty, ain't it?"

"Yeh," I'd say dispiritedly, knowing what was coming.

"That moon," he'd go on, "is easy bright nuff fer us to go out and bring in that hay. C'm on, boy, le's horness up. Makes a fella feel good t' work by moonlight."

I couldn't argue with him. I couldn't tell him that it didn't make *me* feel good to work by moonlight. Many times I wanted to tell him the difference between him and me; I wanted to point out that farm work gave him pleasure because he owned the farm, whereas I hated it and would get pleasure out of seeing his acres sink to China. On those moonlight nights I wanted to tell him that I wasn't interested in bringing in the hay—I wanted to *get* in it.

I did almost everything that's to be done on a farm and hated every moment of it, and my days were made even more unbearable by the presence of Mr. Heffner's son, a kid of about eight. His name was Tommy and he suffered under a psychopathic condition which made him believe that he was superior to me in all departments. He trailed me around from dawn to dusk, taunting me. Suppose we were in a field, and I was walking in a furrow and he was walking on the ridge. Over and over again he'd say, "I'm higher'n you is!" Then suppose he was in the furrow and I was on the ridge. He'd say, "I'm lower'n you is." It strikes me as being sort of a miracle that I never flogged him to death with a can of popcorn.

66

Yet that summer of farming served its salutary purpose. I never again, in all my life, ever threw a brickbat at a lady.

We decided not to stay overnight in Defiance. Somehow things hadn't turned out quite the way I had expected. Maybe this wasn't the town for me to recapture the delightful sensations of boyhood. It would be best, I thought, to get on westward and, especially, to get someplace where I could have my whiskers removed without a letter from my pastor.

Heading for Indiana, we came to another Ohio town and I spotted a barber pole in a crumbling ruin of a building. It was a dark and dirty shop and apparently it was the hangout for the town characters, for half a dozen of them were sitting around the spittoons and the two barber chairs were unoccupied. As I came into the place one of the characters got up and looked me over and I said I wondered if I could get a shave.

"You can," said this character, "pervided you get in this chair here. I ain't able to give you a shave standin' there."

He was a rough individual, this barber, but gentle with the razor, and he didn't stop talking all the time he had me down. He was not, however, talking to me, but to the other men in the shop, and it soon became apparent that he was the town oracle. The others talked, when he permitted it, but whenever his mouth was going they were all quiet and attentive. There was talk about some fellow townsman, known to them all, who had died a few days earlier.

"It was a celeebrial hemmridge," said the barber.

"So I heard," said one of the loafers. "What is one of them celeebrial hemmridges, anyhow? Seems like I heard tell of them."

"Happens in yer head," said the barber. "You got a celeebrial hemmridge, it's like a sorta explosion in your head. You git one and you're a goner. Course I'm speakin' from a *stand* point."

I noticed this speech mannerism throughout his subsequent talk. Whenever he appeared to feel the need to be emphatic about something he always said, "I'm speakin' from a *stand* point."

He was a font of information, this barber, on any and

67

all topics and he enjoyed showing off his knowledge. There are other people like him in the world. Seven hundred and eighty-five million.

"Know how peanuts grow?" he asked his audience as he scraped my chin. There was no reason on earth that I could see why he should have brought up peanuts at that moment, but that's the way he was. He didn't wait for an answer. "The plant," he said, "comes up like any old plant and then some yella blossoms comes on it and outa these yella blossoms comes a stem, size of a broom straw. This stem curves over and keeps growin' and curvin' and then it goes right square into the ground, and right on the end of it, that's where the peanuts grow."

I started to speak through the lather and tell him he was a liar by the clock, but I'm glad I didn't because he had it right.

One of the loafers sat with a fly swatter in his hand and now and then he'd slap a fly off his knee.

" 'y god," said the fly killer, "I can understand why God made almost everything in the world, but what the hell did he have in his mind when he created a dirty no-good fly?"

The barber lifted the razor off my face and turned to stare for a moment at the fly killer. He shook his head from side to side.

"Birch," he said, "that is the dumbest remark I ever heard passed in my life. God had a reason to create flies, and a good reason to boot. Why, man alive, if it wasn't fer flies this country would be fulla unemployment. They'd be bread lines a mile long in the cities and chillren would be starvin' to death. Now look at it this way, Birch. If we didn't have no flies, they wouldn't be no fly-swatter factories, no flypaper factories, no Flit-gun factories, no factories where they make winder screens, and I don't know what all. Think about all the men that wouldn't have no jobs if all them factories wasn't runnin', and they *wouldn't* be runnin' if it wasn't for flies. Right?"

This economic theory was not altogether convincing to the man who had originally challenged the wisdom of fly creation.

68

"You mean to stand there and tell me," he spoke up boldly, "that when God created flies he had it in mind that some- day they would be fly-swatter factories and so on, and give a lot of people work, and solve the unemployment prob- lem?"

"That's what I said," affirmed the barber, "and I'm speakin' from a *stand* point." The discussion was closed. Quiet settled over the room as the loafers digested this re- markable bit of theological reasoning, and the barber finished with me and I prepared to leave. As I went out the door I heard him say, "Know where that guy's from? New York. Betcha anything you wanna bet. I c'd tell from the way his hair was rounded off in the back."

Walking away from the shop, I reached a hand around and felt of the way my hair was rounded off. I hadn't known before that a New York haircut was so distinctive. Then I caught on. My car, with its New York license plate, was parked within full view of the barbershop window. That's one time he wasn't speakin' from a *stand* point.

We were ready now to climb into our car and speed on- ward, new joys always glimmering in the distance. "Just to think," I said to myself, "there are to be six whole weeks of this in this glorious spring weather. What lovely things we shall see!"

I dug into the suitcase devoted to books and notes, just to make sure we had completed our mission in Ohio. And I came up with a clipping which a Mrs. Walker had sent me from Cincinnati. Here it is:

RESISTED WOMAN'S WISHES, MAN SAYS; WINS ACQUITTAL

When Margaret Stanton, 35, attempted to force Lee Thomas, 30, into her bed in her rooms on the third floor at 938 Richmond St. July 14 with a .38 revolver he resisted and in the ensuing scuffle she was shot and killed.

That was the story Thomas told to a jury yesterday at his trial on a charge of second- degree murder. The jury acquitted Thomas later.

Thomas, who is a professional choir singer, testified that the following circumstances preceded the woman's death:

While they were having a few drinks in a café she asked him for money to play "policy." He had money but refused to give any to her. He then took her by taxicab to her door and bade her good night. She insisted that she would need his aid in opening her door so he told the cabdriver to wait.

Thomas went up with the woman and opened her door easily. Then she pulled the revolver out of her purse and, reminding Thomas that he had refused to give money to her, proposed relations with him and ordered him into her bedroom and into her bed. He refused and she threatened him. He finally sat down on the bed and she sat beside him. He then seized her gun hand, they struggled, and in a moment she was shot.

I read it through twice, just to make sure I had it right. Then I leaped to the steering wheel, stepped down hard on the accelerator, and got the hell out of Ohio.

Chapter 6

Indiana is a fascinating state in spite of the sorry beginnings it had. It used to be inhabited by two savage peoples—the Indians and the whites. The Indians didn't have much sense and were inclined to eat each other. It took a long time to bounce them out of the state, but the white settlers who swarmed in from the East and South managed to do it by giving them whisky until they were unable to distinguish between sheep droppings and Shinola.

The early white settlers, according to the books, believed in saving some of the whisky for themselves, arguing that they needed it in summer to ward off sunstroke and in winter to keep themselves warm. At the same time they were a deeply religious people and believed that they had been put on earth for the purpose of telling other people how to run their lives. More than one historian has remarked that, throughout its early history, Indiana was the most narrow and most provincial commonwealth in the country.

The Indians have gone, and while many bigots still inhabit the state, Indiana has shown vast improvement in this direction. Most Hoosiers of my acquaintance are robust and lusty in their attitude toward life, and I even know a few who are willing to let other people live and believe as they choose. There is no more bigotry today in Muncie, Indiana, than there is in Mount Kisco, New York. Perhaps not as much.

A Hoosier loves to sentimentalize over the fact that he *is* a Hoosier, and he also loves to laugh. His humor is earthy; he enjoys telling a dirty story or listening to one. The late Ernie Pyle was as typical a Hoosier as you could find—overflowing with cornbread-and-molasses sentimentality and a guy who loved nothing so much as a session of storytelling in which the stories dealt with barnyard and boudoir. He once predicted that I will die on the gallows.

The earthiness of the ordinary Hoosier is reflected in a document I acquired while I was in Indianapolis. It is a copy of Senate Bill No. 499, which was introduced in the State Senate on February 10, 1939, and reported favorably for passage two days later. I don't know if it ever passed but I do know that it was sent through the hopper.

Senate Bill No. 499 had its origin with a small group of newspaper correspondents and lobbyists. These men were gassing back and forth about the general business of lawmaking and someone suggested that the most fantastic kind of a secondary bill could be introduced in the Legislature and run through without much danger of opposition.

An experiment was decided upon, and someone drew up the bill. It starts out as follows:

"A Bull of an Act levying a service tax on all stallions, jacks, bulls, bears, bucks, rams, dogs, tomcats, and other fertile male animals, the revenue derived to be used to provide mental relief and solaces for all mules, steers, barrows, geldings, and other castrated and/or impotent animal eunuchs.

"Whereas, sufficient consideration never has been given to the sad plight of animal eunuchs, the shocking operation during their tender years, their total loss of one of the major pleasures of life, their keen embarrassment when in sight and hearing of the functioning of their more fortunate fellows, now, therefore, there ort to be a law."

I think I'll stop at this point. There are four pages of it altogether, but it gets a little riskay as it goes along, and there are reasons why I would not consider writing anything that is even slightly off-color.

I am not a Hoosier. For many years when anybody asked me where I came from I usually said Indiana, that being the state in which my folks finally came to rest. I almost got to believing that I was a Hoosier, forgetting the fact that the state of Illinois is alone responsible for me.

During the time I worked on newspapers in New York I got periodic invitations to attend dinners of an organization called the Sons of Indiana, a large and noisy group of men who came out of Indiana and now live in New York. It is not in my nature to join things, so I always backed away from these bids, explaining that I could not rightly be called a son of Indiana. They'd answer this by pointing out that Roy Howard was a member and *he* wasn't born in Indiana. Mr. Howard was born in Guano, Ohio. No, that's not right. Gano, Ohio. When my argument of Illinois origin failed, I told them that I had a long-standing grudge against Indiana —that in the year of my birth the Indiana Legislature, in no joking mood this time, passed a sterilization act to prevent the procreation of criminals, idiots, imbeciles, and rapists, and that I considered this piece of legislation a personal affront.

I did attend one dinner given by the Sons of Indiana. The speaker was Wendell Willkie, but I didn't hear him because my former city editor, B. O. McAnney, and I were off in an anteroom engaged in a lively discussion, Mr. McAnney contending that I was the lousiest, dumbest, infinitive-splittin'est bum he had ever had the misfortune to hire, while I in turn informed him that he was the cruelest, dopiest, fatheadedest tool-of-the-interests I had ever suffered under.

Meanwhile in the big dining room the Hoosiers were indulging in hot reminiscences of their youth in Indiana. Apparently a true Hoosier never succeeds in being anything else but a Hoosier, no matter where destiny leads him; he always enjoys telling the world of the rhapsodies to be found along the Wabash, and the very thought of Indiana would be sufficient to heat up the cockles of his heart, if the heart has any cockles, which is questionable. A cockle, according to Webster, is (1) the darnel; (2) the corn cockle; (3) any of several other plants growing in grainfields, as the cowherb, the corn poppy, cocklebur, etc.; (4) a small gall, resembling the seed of the corn cockle, produced on wheat by the attacks of a nematode worm; (5) any bivalve mollusk of the genus *Cardium* or allied genera, especially the common edible

European species; (6) a shallow boat; (7) a confection of flour and sugar; (8) an earthen pot for cooking; (9) a stove in which biscuit ware is dried; (10) a hop-drying kiln; (11) any mineral occurring in dark long crystals, especially schorl; (12) a pucker, wrinkle, or bulge.

That last one might be stretched to fit. I have known people who had a pucker, wrinkle, or bulge on their hearts, but I think the puckers, wrinkles, or bulges caused them pain, and if those cockles were warmed, it was the heat of pain and not pleasure. I have also known people whose hearts had been attacked by nematode worms, and that might have caused some cockles.

The whole business of heart cockles bothers me, so let us forget about the presence of cockles on the hearts of homesick Hoosiers. Typical of the nostalgic atmosphere to be found at a dinner of the Sons of Indiana are the paragraphs which follow, taken from a speech by Mr. Ford Frick, formerly of Wawaka, now of the National League. Mr. Frick:

It is said that the true Hoosier is born with a jackknife in his pocket, a pine stick in his hand, and a pencil behind his ear. The true Hoosier is suckled on the pap of political expediency; cuts his teeth on the doctrine of self-expression; and, as concerns our generation at least, cherishes as his first and fondest memory the Bryan campaign button that upheld that first infant diaper.

Whether he hails from the murky banks of the Wabash, the peppermint-scented muck lands of Noble County, or the hilled recesses of Old Brown—he is of one mold—changeless and eternal. Who but a Hoosier could gaze on the majesty of the Empire State Building—and feel only nostalgia for the Odd Fellows Hall of his youth and the Pythian Temple of his boyhood? Who but a Hoosier could listen to the strains of a great symphony orchestra and translate them unconsciously into terms of the barn-dance fiddler? Or, listening to the philippics of a modern Demosthenes, feel only the disappointment of a disillusioned man who has been weaned on the superior oratory of a Beveridge or the friendly phrases of our Tall Sycamore of the Wabash? Who but a Hoosier, I ask you, could transplant to the heart of New York the humble community box supper—and make it take place as a social event and an epicurean accomplishment?

Inspiring, ain't it! And I ask you to please take note of one important fact—Mr. Frick doesn't once hint at that lovely Indiana institution, the pool hall.

In the days of my youth I made an earnest effort to follow in the footsteps of my illustrious father by spending a good portion of my time hanging around poolrooms. I never became really expert with the cue stick, but over a period of years I absorbed much of the wholesome atmosphere that is to be found in small-town pool halls and even tried to chew tobacco once.

Some readers might get the impression from this book that I am trying to suggest that there has never been any nostalgia in me; if so, the picture is false. When a fellow gets into the neighborhood of forty and begins to creak at the hubs little nostalgic urges are bound to assault him. In my case I freely admit that I once got homesick for the poolrooms of Indiana.

Maybe Mr. Frick and the others did their boyhood frolicking at the Odd Fellows Hall, but I didn't. In years gone by, whenever I developed a vague yearning for a return to the idyllic days, I would hear the click of pool balls and the soft musical plash on the rims of the goboons, and into my nostrils would come the long-gone aroma—the alluring odor of an Indiana poolroom, of which there is no equal anywhere in New York City unless it be the men's rooms in the subway station.

I recall one afternoon in which I was bumbling around amid the frightening towers of Rockefeller Center when I got to thinking about poolrooms. New York, it is said, has everything—absolutely everything—if you know how to find it. The urge was on me to recapture the fine tingle of youth, so I steered for Sixth Avenue and soon spotted a sign that said "Billiards." I walked up one flight and entered a spacious room filled with light, which was wrong, and also filled with pool and billiard tables.

One of the first things I saw was a woman. Then I saw another woman. And after that I saw *four* women. One of the ladies was shooting a game of billiards with a man. Some distance away four young women were engaged in a grim game of straight pool. And the other woman I saw, a trim blonde, was wearing a white uniform. If she had ever entered a poolroom of my youth she would have departed, ultimately, with enough to keep her talking the rest of her life.

This blonde in uniform came swishing past me and went through a door at the far end of the room. Over this door was a sign which said, "Bridge."

I was a trifle stunned, but I crossed over and went through the door into a room where about thirty men and women were sitting at tables playing cards. The blonde came up to me and I quickly told her that I was no bridge player.

"Gin rummy?" she asked. I said no. "Pinochle?" No. I said I wanted to talk to the owner or manager of the place. She went away and soon came back with a little man who was the manager. I cross-examined him about the decline of iniquity in the poolroom. He said he was making a great effort to attract the female trade.

"Over there," he said, "you see a man and his wife playing billiards. And you can see the four ladies playing pool. I try to make the place attractive to dames. You fill the place up with dames and you don't have any swearing and cussing, not even loud talk. No fights, not even arguments. The men who come in here are all high class—doctors, lawyers, radio commentators, actors—so naturally the ladies who are in here are also high class. I have found that if an intelligent high-class lady shoots a couple games of pool, she's gonna shoot plenty pool from then on. I expect to see the day when there will be more ladies in here than men, all the time."

I heaved. I mean I heaved a sigh. I thanked him and went to the head of the stairs. At the door I turned around because a strong temptation had come upon me. I wanted to spit on the floor and then run, but I didn't. I just went away, and for the remainder of that day I was really homesick for Indiana.

At the time the Ford Fricks were sitting in the Odd Fellows Hall whittling on pine sticks, I was shooting craps in a roadhouse near Jeffersonville while a thug with a sawed-off shotgun sat on a little balcony overhead and watched the door, ready to deal with any gangsters who might, and frequently did, come along to hijack the joint. At the time Ford Frick himself was in New York listening to the strains of a

great symphony orchestra and translating them unconsciously into terms of the barn-dance fiddler, I was sitting
in a restaurant in Ybor City, Florida, drinking bootleg
whisky out of a coffee cup in preparation for an evening of
gambling at the dog track.

You see, in my case, how impossible it is to create a
Hoosier out of the material at hand. I just don't seem to fit.
The things that other people remember and yearn for when
they leave the Midwest mean little or nothing to me. At no
point in my life did I ever stir apple butter or soap. Never
did I ever look for water with a willow wand. I had a few
freckles when I was a kid, but I never washed them with
stump water. I killed a toad or two as a boy, but my cow

77

didn't give bloody milk in consequence. I've smelled new-mown hay and bread in the oven and apple blossoms and all that, but I never considered those smells to be extra-special; I once got a whiff of a beautiful woman in the Stork Club in New York City and, to me, she smelled better than all the hay that has been new-mown since the lifetime of Adam's neglected nigh ox. Let the frost get on the punkin and let the fodder get in the shock but don't bother me about it. I've got trouble enough trying to pick a winner at Belmont.

For a writing man it is supposed to be a salutary circumstance if you come from Indiana. The state has turned out a lot of famous authors, from Edward Eggleston down to Elmer Davis. The big names, of course, are James Whitcomb Riley, Booth Tarkington, Meredith Nicholson, George Ade, Theodore Dreiser, and Lloyd Douglas.

All my life I've been hearing this talk about the great literary traditions of Indiana. During the last hour I've been taking a quick course in the subject. I beg to report that:

Edward Eggleston's stuff is generally considered to be authentic and good, and nobody reads it.

James Whitcomb Riley, by critical standards, is head-and-shoulders above Edgar Guest, but not very big head-and-shoulders.

Lew Wallace was okay.

A Hoosier named Will Carleton wrote *Over the Hill to the Poorhouse.*

Ambrose Bierce lived much of his early life in Indiana but didn't like it and went West before he found out he knew how to write.

Lloyd C. Douglas was born and raised and preached in Indiana, and his books sell in spite of the devil.

Charles Major of Indiana wrote *When Knighthood Was in Flower* and *Dorothy Vernon of Haddon Hall.*

A man named Thomas Say, of New Harmony, turned out a book titled *American Conchology, or Description of the Shells of North America, Illustrated by Colored Figures from Original Drawings Executed from Nature.* I'm sorry he beat me to that title.

John Hay, who became a big shot in Washington, was a

novelist, poet, and one of Lincoln's biographers. After he went East he disowned Indiana, which he called "barbarous."

A woman named Ellsworth in Lafayette was author of a famous work. It seems that when Morse was getting all set to invent the telegraph, he tipped Miss Ellsworth off about it and told her that when he got the thing in working order he'd let her make up the first message to be transmitted. I don't know why he did this, but he did, and I can visualize Miss Ellsworth fussing her head off over the problem. Finally she came up with the line, "What hath God wrought?" and sent it on to Morse and he used it, although I imagine he was a mite disappointed in it, figuring that he had wrought a little bit himself.

Joaquin Miller, the Pacific Coast poet, was born in Indiana. He's the one who considered his toenails to be immortal.

When Dreiser took his Hoosier Holiday and got to Indianapolis he told how he had driven past the home of James Whitcomb Riley, and how he had been tempted to go in and pay his respects, but he didn't do it because he had heard that Riley didn't approve of the Dreiser kind of literature. Dreiser seemed to be hurt about this and felt sad about it. If it had been me, I'd have marched right into the old jerk's house and hit him in the puss with a frosted punkin. Except that I think he would have approved of *my* kind of literature.

At one point in our rambles over Indiana we passed through Greenfield, the town of Riley's origin, but we didn't bother calling at the Riley homestead (admission 25 cents) for the reason that its former occupant didn't approve of Theodore Dreiser and for the further reason that he wore glasses with a black ribbon attached. Instead we hurried along to the nearby community of Knightstown, attracted by a story we found in the *Indiana Guide*. There was a man named William Herschell who came from another part of the state and who also wrote poetry. I don't know what he was doing in the neighborhood of Knightstown; maybe he was poaching on Riley's grounds, trying to get some of the Riley feeling into his own poems by creeping up within a dozen miles of the Ole Swimmin' Hole and Little Orphant Annie's house. This Herschell was thumping around out east of Knightstown, where the pastoral scenes are nice, when he came upon an old man fishing in the Blue River. According to Herschell, this old man took his eyes off his bobber, waved an arm around the horizon, and exclaimed, "Ain't God good to Indianny?" To Herschell this was a beautiful sentiment beautifully put, so he hauled off and wrote a poem called *Ain't God Good to Indiana?* The folks around Knightstown are proud of the fact that their countryside inspired that poem, and they'll tell you about it if you'll stand still long enough, and if they happen to think of it they'll also mention that Knightstown was the birthplace of a feller named Charles A. Beard who went East and wrote some history books or somethin'.

But enough about literary Indiana for the time being. We'll come back to it later.

Chapter 7

As we approached Huntington, the town where I spent the concluding years of my boyhood, it started to rain. Now why did I say it that way, It started to rain? What started to rain? Doesn't seem to make sense. Yet that's the way everybody says it and writes it. It's cold out. What's cold out. It. What is IT? I hate to quarrel with my own language, but the more words a person puts down on paper the more he recognizes the goofiness of many widely used expressions. Once upon a time. What does that mean? How can a *once* get up astraddle of a time, and become a *once* upon a *time?* Well, anyway, whatever *it* was, or is, *it* started to rain. We were perhaps five miles out of Huntington, and in something like thirty seconds I was back in my childhood again. There was an overture done in hailstones as big as tit eggs. Another example of language confusion: a tit is a bird. The hailstones rattled and banged against the Plymouth for a few minutes and then the sky got itself organized, flexed its thunderheads, took a deep breath, and let go. I hadn't seen water come down like that since I left the Midwest. It couldn't properly be called rain because solid water cannot go pitter-patter. Inside the car, pulled up at the side of the highway, we had the sensation of imminent drowning, as though we had suddenly been trapped in a Hoosier Red Sea, like Caesar or Odyssey or Job's turkey or whoever it was. All traffic ceased, and the deluge washed my car cleaner than I myself ever washed it, saving me a dollar and a half. Ain't God good to former Egyptians?

When it was over I half expected to see rescuers coming across the cornfield in rowboats; instead everyone along the road picked up where he had left off and nobody appeared to be excited. A meteorological ruction of that nature is commonplace, but it had been so long since I had experienced a real cloudburst that it served to goose my psyche. The way that water came down, I had a feeling that I was in my early teens, and I had another feeling that I could get out of the car and swim the rest of the way into Huntington, twenty feet above the highway.

We went on into Huntington, a municipality of around fifteen thousand immortal souls. The town is bisected by the Little Wabash River and doesn't have a very exciting history although it has been in existence since the 1820s. A couple of brothers from Tennessee named Helvey founded the original village which the Indians called Wepechaangange which, loosely translated, means, "Whoopee, the chain gang!" The Helvey brothers apparently didn't like the name Wepechaangange, probably because they couldn't pronounce it, and, anyway, they were picaresque, poetic fellows, so they gave their new village the romantic name of Section 15, Town 28 North, Range 9, Ind. They built a two-story tavern out of logs and then looked around for a sucker. They found one in the person of General John Tipton, hero of a twenty-minute battle against the Indians on the White River.

This General Tipton had one thing in common with the human race: he enjoyed hearing the music of his own name, and when he helped settle another village on the White River some years earlier, he talked the folks into calling it Tiptonia. This village grew rapidly and in 1821 was big enough to become a county seat. The general offered to donate thirty acres of his land to the county, for public buildings and the like, provided the town retain the name of Tiptonia. The county commissioners agreed to this deal. General Tipton signed over his thirty acres, the county commissioners said thanks, and then the county commissioners named the town Columbus. Lumping this evidence together, I would say that it suggests General Tipton was not admired overmuch. He was so sore about the double cross that he lit out for Logansport and built himself a mansion to sulk in. After a while he got restless and started looking around for another place where he might start a town with better luck. He finally decided that this Wepechaangange up on the Little Wabash had possibilities, might ultimately become a prosperous community well equipped with deep-freeze units and diathermy machines. So he bought the land from the Helvey brothers.

General Tipton lived on in Logansport and sent a Captain Elias Murray to be his representative in running the affairs of Section 15, Town 28 North, Range 9. I don't have any information about the specific instructions he gave Captain Murray, but on the basis of past performance I should imagine he told the captain to rename the place Tipton, or Tiptonia, or Tiptoe. If he did, Captain Murray gave him the same treatment that he got from the commissioners in Columbus. Captain Murray was a nephew of Samuel Huntington of Connecticut, one of the signers of the Declaration of Independence, so he named the town Huntington.

I went into hiding at the home of my mother when I arrived in Huntington since I was skittish about the town and fearful that I might be slugged by a vestryman if I appeared on the streets. One of the first things I learned was that during the last year a delegation of high-school boys had called on my mother with a piece of information which they wanted transmitted to me. They said that two different teachers, both male (to all appearances), had made quite violent attacks on me. One of them had addressed his class as follows:

"We hear a great deal about the seriousness of the paper shortage these days. I have a suggestion to make to the government. A good way to save paper would be to stop the publication of books by a person named H. Allen Smith, who seems to have lived in this city at one time. He is a disgrace to Huntington and his publishers should long ago have stopped circulating his vile writings."

Later on the second teacher took up the cudgels, telling his students that he was in an evil humor this morning for a reason—that he had been up late the night before reading one of my books and that he had become so infuriated at it that he had thrown it clear across the room and then gone over and stomped on it.

The informal committee of students told my mother they thought she should tell me about these incidents, so I could write something about them in one of my future books.

Why, boys, I wouldn't want to do a thing like that! After all, those teachers are educated people, and I'm not; therefore I'm in no position to dispute with them. As it happens, I feel a certain tenderness toward them, a sense of pity for them, and I wish it were in my power to help them in some way. I wouldn't even know them if I saw them, but if I did, if I met one of them on the street, I'd step up to him with my heart full of kindliness. I'd speak gently to him, to throw him off his guard, and then I'd slap him in the face with a sock loaded with a pound and a half of rancid chicken livers.

After the first day I got up my courage and began venturing out. Huntington is a bustling little city, and the automobile traffic on Jefferson Street was heavier, I think, than any traffic I ever drove through on the island of Manhattan. I wandered around the main part of town for quite a spell and nobody paid any attention to me except certain pedestrians who seemed to be horrified by the repulsive checkered shirt I had on. I stopped in a butcher shop to pick up an order of meat for the house, and I was walking down the main street toward my car when I heard my name called out above the traffic noises. I turned around and a policeman was running toward me. I grew faint and my kneecaps began to jiggle. It was ever thus in the old days in Huntington— every time I turned around a cop was coming at me. I stood there, my hands full of meat, wondering if it was an old indictment, some charge that had been standing against me for twenty-odd years. I cringed a little as the cop came up to me. He said:

"Godamighty! You almost got away from me! Listen, pal, I heard you were in town and I happened to be in that butcher shop and the butcher told me who you were. I've read all your books, every durn one of 'em, and brother I love 'em. I wanna shake your hand."

I shook his hand and ceased shaking all over and felt real good, but the experience had weakened me physically, so I went home and went to bed for a while.

Subsequently I drove around town, revisiting the halcyon scenes of my boyhood. I peeped through the window of the barbershop where I shined shoes and swept up old hair just prior to getting a job on a newspaper. I went up to the building which had housed that newspaper, the Huntington *Press*. The paper had long since been merged with the *Herald*, and the *Herald-Press* is now published down near the river's edge. And as Dreiser would have done it I stood across the street and gazed at the old *Press* building and searched my soul for sadness.

A strange remembrance forced its way into my mind. I

remembered that I was sitting in the newsroom on the second floor of this building one slow evening reading a magazine containing what purported to be confessions—written confessions of people who had been guilty of wrong-doing, mostly with their clothes off. I remembered opening the magazine to a page where one of the confessions began and seeing the heading over the article, "Her Husband Loved Her But——" In my own peculiar way I thought there was something funny about that headline, and I wondered if the man who wrote it was a dealer in double-entendre or if he just hit upon the thing by accident.

My stream of consciousness took me completely away from the old building, for the memory of that headline jogged my thoughts back to a letter I got from a soldier during the war. He wrote:

"I wonder if you would be able to tell me what part of a woman is her yet. We have been puzzled about it out here in the Philippines. We know that a woman has got a yet, but what is it? The reason we know it is that we heard an officer talking the other day. He said that there was a girl in Manila who had been shot recently and the bullet was in her yet. Please tell us what it is."

I didn't quite know how to answer that letter. I mentioned it to my agent and he gave the matter a few moments thought and then he said he knew a way for me to answer it.

"Tell them," he said, "that a woman's yet is the same as her now."

"And what is her now?"

"Oh, you know," he said. "Don't you remember—I Wonder Who's Kissing Her Now?"

Thinking of these things, I simply couldn't get melancholy about the old days at the *Press*. Some pictures came back to me . . . Homer Ormsby, the publisher, pacing the floor for hours, thinking up editorials. He is now in his seventies and is mayor of Arcadia, California. But most of the things I could remember I've written about already and there is little sadness in any of them. I gave up and started out for Idle Hour.

Idle Hour was a resort a couple of miles east of town, and I spent many a busy hour at Idle Hour. A dance hall stood near the lip of an old quarry, and the quarry was filled with nice clean water and was so deep in places that the best divers had never found bottom. There were diving towers and springboards and floats and a few rowboats and it was a fine place to swim and dive. At night, though, the big attraction was the dance hall, which brought people from as far away as Fort Wayne. Good orchestras, by the standards of the day, were engaged and for the most part played fast jazz tunes which fitted the current style of dancing. To dance, in those days, meant to bob up and down at a rapid rate while the band played, say, "Chicago, Chicago, that toddlin' town!" just as pell-mell as it could. If you have read the saga of Studs Lonigan by James T. Farrell you will recall the kind of dancing old Studs went in for in Chicago. We also had quite a bit of that at Idle Hour. A fella always knew which girls would put up with it and which wouldn't. I participated to the best of my small abilities.

Since it had been my custom to spend all my spare time at Idle Hour, either swimming or dancing, a heavy nostalgia came upon me when I headed east to see the place again. I drove my wife out, telling her on the way of the glorious days and nights I had spent at Idle Hour and of the things I did there, not mentioning the Lonigan business. We had gone about five miles when I realized that I was too far out and concluded that my memory was not too good, that I had taken the wrong road. I turned the car around and started back, and after a while I saw it, off to the right of the road. The banks of the old quarry were grown thick with brush and weeds and the water itself was barely visible from the highway. The dance hall was gone—everything was gone, but there was a rectangular clearing where the dance hall had been, and a few remnants of the foundations, and smack in the middle of that rectangle was an old nanny goat, placidly lying on that sacred ground and chewing a vulgar cud. This is the point where, I think, I came the nearest to feeling real sad. I was on the verge of heartbreak when my wife, gesturing toward the goat, remarked:

"Well, one of your old girl friends is left, anyway."

A cruel thrust! Especially when you consider that I saved her from marrying a hapless fellow in Florida, a guy who had nothing but a million dollars, two Cadillacs, a yacht, and a plantation.

It happens that in the period just before I left Huntington I was a society boy. I was permitted to run with the sons and daughters of the hot maunde. I dated the daughters of rich people and was invited to all the parties and dances they gave. It may have been my good looks and poise, and then again it may have been the fact that I worked on the local newspaper and always gave everyone in my crowd extensive write-ups.

I saw none of these people on my return but I picked up gossip about them. What I found in Huntington I also found in other towns I had known. A quarter of a century can effect some wondrous social alterations. In many cases the society people of my time had gone to the dogs, lost their money and their fine homes. Some of the mighty who had fallen turned to sinful pursuits when their day of glory was done; others had gone to work—the barons become vassals. This leveling process worked in both directions, of course, and I heard of people who were impecunious and raffish in my day who now sat at shiny desks and bellowed orders at the hired help.

Huntington had two fraternities when I lived there. These Greek-letter groups were not connected with any schools, although I've been told they had their origins in high schools. Each fraternity had its clubrooms, and the principal function of the membership seemed to be the giving of fancy dances and the flailing of pledges across the britches with heavy paddles. If you were a young fellow in Huntington and didn't become associated with one or the other of these fraternities you simply were nobody. Well, I got pledged to one of them. I suppose it was because of the way I stood in with the society group. But while I was pledged I never achieved full knighthood. Looking back on it now, I think those town sports took me in simply as a practice field for bottom-blasting. Every time I walked into those clubrooms one of the older guys would say, "All right, half-wit, get over that chair." I had to do it or lose my franchise. I had to lay myself over a big leather chair in a position that would make my pants tight across the seat, and how they used to lay it on! It is a physiological marvel that I am not crippled as a result of that punishment. But I stood it, and stood up for many meals.

There came the time when the current pledges were to be initiated, the night on which they would be awarded full membership and the privilege of beating later pledges across the behinds. The first thing they gave me to do was a window-counting job. I had to go to the extreme north end of Jefferson Street, which is the town's main thoroughfare. I was to count every window, every pane of glass, that faced on Jefferson Street, whether it be in a house or a store. The street must be a couple of miles long, but I went at the job with eagerness and industry. I was warned that the initiation committee knew the exact number of windows on the street and that if I made an error I would not get into the fraternity. When I finally arrived at the clubrooms and announced my findings, there was considerable argument as to the accuracy of my count. Two men supported me and one was against me, and the one who was against me (my sister had thrown him over for another guy a year or so earlier) grudgingly settled for the privilege of assaulting my buttocks with twenty cobs.

Having passed the window test by the skin of my, shall we say teeth, they gave me a new assignment. A coonskin cap was placed on my head and an alarm clock was hung around my neck by a heavy cord. I was escorted to the town's chief intersection, Market and Jefferson. All this beautiful ceremony, I should explain, took place on a Saturday night, and the town was crowded with farmers and people from outlying villages. At the intersection a tall lamppost was pointed out to me and I was told to shinny up this post once every five minutes and, on reaching a point where I could touch the light globe with my hand, I was to cry out at the top of my voice, "Coo-koo!" ten times. I was to keep this up until I had been up the pole twenty-five times and cried "Coo-koo!" two hundred and fifty times.

My feet and legs were killing me from that window-counting job and the paddle whacks had been delivered with such hateful vigor that I was almost raw there, but I went at the lamppost manfully. In ten minutes a large crowd had

89

gathered. Most of the onlookers had no idea what was going on and, being rural-routers, wouldn't have understood the shining symbolism even if they had been told.

The crowd was overflowing onto the pavement by the time a half hour of coo-kooing had passed, and then old John Johnson, the cop, arrived. He began shooing people on their way, but most of them refused to budge, never having seen anything quite like this before. Then he stood off and watched me climb the post and do my act. He was waiting for me when I came down.

"I might of known," he said, "it would be you. Where'd you get it?"

"Get what?"

"Th' booze. C'm on, where'd you get it?"

I explained to him that I was not drunk, and he leaned forward and had a sniff at my breath.

"Well, then," he said, "you been takin' dope."

At length I succeeded in convincing him that I was being initiated into full and splendid membership in the fraternity.

"Oh," he said with that fine sarcasm which all policemen command, "so you're bein' initiated. That's all right with me, except if you go up that pole again, I run you in for incitin' to riot, disturbin' th' peace, blockin' traffic, and insanity. Go somewheres out in the country and climb a tree like a goddam fool if you want to, but don't go up that pole no more."

Dejectedly I made my way to the clubrooms and reported what had happened.

"Get the hell back there," the committee ordered, "and climb that pole and finish the assignment."

"But what about John Johnson?"

"Defy him."

"He said he'd pinch me."

"You been pinched before. Get going."

I returned to the corner to find that the crowd had dispersed, but old John Johnson was still there. He remained obdurate. If I shinnied up that pole just one more time, I'd spend the night in jail. Again I went back to the clubrooms and again I found no sympathy. The man who had given me the twenty cobs began yelling for my scalp and sought

support for a project in which I was to be thrown down the stairs. Sore of body, weak of limb, hoarse of voice, I now got a little hysterical and did a little yelling of my own and worked some profanity into it. I saw my enemy start for the corner of the room to get the heavy paddle, and he was shouting how this time he was going to beat it off of me. At that moment all the yearning for blessed brotherhood went out of me. I took off the coonskin cap and threw it at him. I took off the alarm clock and dashed it against a wall. I announced in a loud voice that every member of the fraternity was close kin to a mama dog, and then I turned and ran out of the place before they could get their hands on me. Those guys never did like me after that, and I think it was a good thing that within a few months I left Huntington under more clouds than the United States Weather Bureau has in its handbook for beginners.

I visited that lamppost, and it stirred memories but no feeling of regret that the olden times were gone. I stood there, leaning against the front of a drugstore, and the only emotion I was able to raise couldn't properly be called an emotion, since it was nothing more than a tingling sensation in the area where the cobs were laid on. I wondered if Theodore Dreiser had ever been given any cobs or if he had ever clumb a lamppost and made coo-koo noises. Then I crossed the street to visit a man named Arthur H. Sapp. Yes, I said Arthur H. Sapp.

For a great many years Arthur H. Sapp was Huntington's most prominent citizen. He was a lawyer with state-wide civic interests, and shortly after I left Huntington, back in the 1920s, he became the president of Rotary International. He was such a big man that even in the days when I was a reporter in Huntington I had never set eyes on him. I went to call on him now because he had represented me, indirectly, in a real-estate deal. I might as well confess at this point that I own part of Whoopee-the-Chain-Gang; not much of it, but a lovely bit of land best described as part of lots fourteen and fifteen in William Taylor's Subdivision of a part of the east half of the northeast quarter of section twenty-two, township twenty-eight north, range nine east in the city of Huntington, Indiana, commencing at the south-east corner of lot fourteen, thence west on the south line of said lot, sixty-two and one half feet, thence north sixty-five feet, thence east sixty-two and one half feet to the east line of said lot number fifteen, thence south sixty-five feet to the place of beginning. Sounds like a nice spot for a vacation, doesn't it?

I wanted to ask Mr. Sapp to continue representing me in the event I ever needed it. He turned out to be a nice old man occupying an office in which, I imagine, Abraham Lincoln once slept. He was a lawyer and a Rotarian, so I didn't dispute him when he told me that he remembered me well, and always had liked me, and always figured I'd get ahead in the world. We talked over my small business affairs, and then when I got up to go he found a piece of paper and a pen and asked me for my autograph. Recognition at last! And from Arthur H. Sapp! And after I had signed my name for him he told me that if I didn't have an automobile I could use his car during my stay in Huntington. I all but embraced him after that, and it is with regret that I must report that he died a few months later.

The following morning we set out for Indianapolis, pronounced Indy-napluss.

Chapter 8

Before we started on this trip we decided that we would not stay in the homes of any relatives, that in every town we visited we would live in a local hotel.

Both my wife and I have strong feelings on this point. Staying at the homes of relatives and friends generally makes for acute discomfort for all concerned. A housewife, when she hits the road, should be done with the worries of housework until she gets back home. And unless her relatives are wealthy and keep a stable of hired help, she's going to do housework along the way. It's inevitable unless she happens to be both lazy and indifferent to the opinion of her kinfolks.

Suppose you go to visit relatives in, say, Cedar Rapids. A bedroom is assigned to you, if a spare is available. Or it may be that somebody in the family gives up his or her room and sleeps on the divan in the living room, or on a pallet, or in the attic, or the basement, or even goes over to the neighbor's where they have a spare bedroom. I, for one, would not be a bit comfortable in such circumstances, knowing that I had bounced someone out of his bed.

Now. You are in Cousin Joe's comfortable bed and Cousin Joe is strung up between two trees in the side yard, occupying a hammock. You get up in the morning. A conscientious woman, a woman with just a snifter of pride, is going to spread up the bed, and not leave it to Aunt Myrtle, who certainly has enough to do with the cooking. So the wife of the visiting team sets to work. Downstairs Aunt Myrtle is fixing breakfast—so the wife hurries down and a cheerful colloquy follows. Like this:

WIFE: "I'll set the table."

AUNT: "Oh no you *will* not! You march right into that living room and set yourself down. Things'll be ready in a jiffy."

WIFE: "Now, Aunt Myrtle, I insist. Here, let me slice the baloney."

AUNT: "Put that knife down! Now scat outa here! Go on in and turn on the radio. The morning paper's on the piano."

The wrangling goes on all day. After breakfast the visitor just *insists* on helping clear the table and washing or wiping (nowadays called "drying") the dishes, and there are two more meals to go, with the action and dialogue repeated through every operation connected with the cooking and serving of them.

The visiting wife certainly doesn't *want* to spread up the bed or set the table or slice the baloney or help with the dishes; she'd far, far rather be in a comfortable hotel, having breakfast in her room—a breakfast that wouldn't include sliced baloney; having people come and get the dishes and carry them away, and more people come and spread up the bed and empty the ash trays and sweep the floor and clean up the bathroom—a bathroom which is her own for the time being, where she has a reasonable chance of gaining admittance. She has gone on a trip to escape from housework, to have a vacation from it, and here she is at Aunt Myrtle's working most of the day because it is polite to do so, traditionally polite, and she'd be looked upon as a poor wife, a woman who hadn't been properly fetched up, if she didn't do it. And Aunt Myrtle—she, too, is wishing secretly that these people were at the hotel because they've upset the entire household, and Joe will probably catch his death in that hammock, and that slovenly bum from New York simply insists on dropping cigarette ashes on the carpets and uses up all the hot water taking shower baths so a body can't get the dishes washed, and My God the grocery bill I'm gonna have after this is over. But Aunt Myrtle is bound by convention, too, and a week ago was bellowing her insistence that they stay at her home, and even said she didn't want them to come to Cedar Rapids if they insulted her by staying in a hotel. Her motive, of course, and the motives of all who resemble her, was a simple one. What would the neighbors say if her relatives came to town and stayed in a hotel!

We wrote to all relatives whose towns we expected to visit and told them in strongly worded prose how we felt about it, and said we would strike their towns off our itinerary if we couldn't stay in hotels.

Such a ruckus as followed! Such whooping and hollering and hysterical indignation! We had insulted them! My mother and my wife's mother had extensive conniptions and mentioned all the pain and sorrow they had suffered in bearing us and bringing us up. The others wrote letters of impassioned protest, and some even telephoned long distance to say they'd never heard of such a thing in their lives. Finally we decided to yield in the case of the mothers, but nowhere else.

So far as Indianapolis was concerned, we reckoned without the knowledge that we would be there during the city's biggest week—the time of the 500-mile Speedway race. It was impossible to get a hotel room anywhere in the city, so we had to compromise again and stay at the home of my sister. Fortunately she lives in a big house and actually had a spare bedroom, with bath, so it was all right.

She was having her troubles, although we didn't know about them until we were settled in her home. Something was wrong with the electric pump in the basement so that hot water came through the faucets in the tiniest of trickles; and outdoors, on the big front lawn, the drainage system had become clogged and a man was at work trying to fix it.

Inasmuch as I am a property owner and since I have a drainage system that will someday get clogged, I went down across the lawn to witness the repair work. The drainage expert was a husky fellow with a round, cheerful, florid face, and he had a small machine going on the lawn. He told me it was a roto-rooter. It was an electrically driven contraption operating on the principle of a plumber's snake. The man explained that roots often force their way between sections of drainage pipe, obstructing the flow, and that in his belief that was the trouble in this case and he already had the head of his roto-rooter working some thirty feet from the point where it entered the ground. He was sweating furiously and he had the hiccups. My chief reason, in fact, for bringing him into this story is to tell about those hiccups. Whenever he hiccuped he shook the earth and, hearing those mighty yerps, it occurred to me that among its other attractions the Midwest certainly excels in hiccups. When a Midwesterner gets the hiccups he doesn't do any halfway job about it. When I lived in the Midwest I used to get them occasionally, and I can remember the power and the glory of them. Each hiccup came close to tearing off my head. After I moved away to other sections of the country I still got hiccups, but they were feeble and had no character to them. Medical science may dispute me on this, but the fact remains that I hadn't heard such bone-rattling hiccups as this roto-rooter engineer was giving off since I had left Indiana. His diaphragm would contract suddenly, his glottis would close, the air would rush into his mouth and bang up against that closed glottis, and a sound would emerge that frightened the woodpeckers in the sycamore trees and stunned moles. The roto-rooter was chugging noisily, yet that man's hiccups could be heard at the back of the house fifty yards away. Through it all he retained the most cheerful aspect, and the fact that he didn't seem to consider anything wrong bolsters my argument that a Midwestern hiccup is without a peer in the land. He didn't even seem aware of the fact that he had the hiccups, despite the fact that each tremendous yerp rattled the change in his pants pocket. He could have, I felt, withdrawn that thirty feet of roto-rooter from the drainpipe, put his face down to the opening, hiccuped once, and blown out roots a block and a half up the road.

My sister has three children, consisting of a pair of boys called Pat and Mike and a girl of high-school caliber called Donna Jean. My sister also has a household problem which I myself have at home—the way of a high-school girl with a telephone. My own telephone problem is wrapped up in the person of my daughter, who can talk to one of her friends for an hour and a quarter without saying anything, and does so evening after evening.

A couple of years back I thought I had found a solution to the thing. I consulted an electrician and found that it would be a simple operation to tap my phone and run a wire from it to the radio loud-speaker in the living room. Then when my daughter began one of her marathon chats, I'd simply flip a switch and her voice and the voice of the wobblehead with whom she was talking would come into the room for everyone to hear. I figured such a setup would reduce her telephone conversations to essentials, of which there are none. I was all ready to order the hookup made when I found out that it is against the law to tap a telephone, even the one in your own house. The manager of the telephone company told me he was happy such a law existed. He said my electrician had told about my scheme around town and the telephone company was geting requests from scores of parents of teen-age girls—requests for permission to tap their own phones.

The Sullivans of Indianapolis have Donna Jean's telephoning to contend with and they also have Pat's, so that for a good part of the time the household is cut off from communication with the outside world. I witnessed one of Pat's sessions at the phone and it was heart-warming. Pat was captain of the baseball team at the Catholic school he attends. One evening after dinner he went to the phone and began dialing numbers. He was reasonably abrupt and to the point once he got the party he was calling. He called about twenty members of the baseball squad and in business-like fashion identified himself and then said that there would be practice the following day. Having made all these calls, he now dialed the number of the priest who coached the ball team and I heard him say:

"I've called all the boys, Father. Told 'em to be on hand tomorrow morning at ten. How's that? Oh. Sure, I'll take care of it."

He hung up and started dialing again. It seems that the coach had told him there *wouldn't* be practice tomorrow, and now Pat went down the list of twenty players, calling each one with the news.

Pat confused and embarrassed me in another direction. Quite a few of his friends stopped by to see him during my stay at his house, and he had a peculiar method of introducing me. There was a copy of one of my books on a coffee table in the living room. On the back of the jacket were some blurbs put there by the publisher—excerpts from reviews, flattering remarks made by logrollers. Whenever Pat brought one of his friends into the room he'd first pick up the book, glance at the blurbs on the back, then say, "Joe, meet my uncle. He's a screwball." Or, "Eddie, I want you to meet my uncle. He's another Mark Twain." Or, "Bill, this is my uncle. He gives off shocking sparks, only you can't see 'em."

No author can truthfully say that he has reached the peak of success until the day comes when a large department store invites him to appear in person at an autographing party. From the time when I first produced a book I looked forward to that great day of recognition, and after seven long years it came—in Indianapolis.

The autographing party was scheduled for a Friday and there were ads about it in the local papers: "Come in and meet H. Allen Smith. Mr. Smith will autograph his books from 3 to 5 on the main floor."

It made me feel fairly important. At the same time I was more than a little apprehensive. I had trouble getting my car parked, and it was after three o'clock when I found myself approaching the store. I noted with satisfaction that the crowds were not yet overflowing into the street—perhaps the madness and rioting would not come until after four o'clock. I was slightly chagrined to find no evidence of police reserves. Really! These people in Indiana! Back in New York we know how to handle a situation like this! Well, they'd find out when this mob got out of hand! I began to feel uncomfortable. It was a hot day and it would be rough on me physically. I decided that promptly at five o'clock I'd lay down my pen and announce firmly that I would not sign another book for ten thousand dollars.

I hurried into the store and found the book department. No mob. No crowd. Nobody. Very likely they were holding

99

the people behind heavy ropes back in some other department. I found my way to the manager's office.

He was very pleasant. "All ready for the grind?" he smiled. I assured him I was ready for anything. He then escorted me to a long table in the center of the book department. Several hundred copies of my books were stacked on this table. There was a chair, a desk pen, a blotter, and an ash tray.

I sat down and loosened my collar. The manager brought over his assistant and introduced her. Then he brought over some of his clerks and introduced them. After that he scanned the horizon, a worried look on his face. Finally he leaned down and said: "You know, we never can tell what will happen at these shindigs."

"Sure," I said. "I know." Just as if I had been through a thousand department-store campaigns.

A couple of women came by. They looked at me and at the piles of books. Then they looked at each other and shrugged, and moved on—probably headed for the drug department to buy rat poison to feed to their husbands.

The manager was embarrassed and tried to divert me. He told me about a local woman who wrote books and who always had an autographing party after each book was published.

"She insists," he said, "on signing her books with gray ink, and it has to be a particular shade of gray. We had to hold up the proceedings over an hour one day when she ran out of ink and we couldn't find the shade of gray she used. She refused to sign without it, and all the customers were getting sore."

Somehow it didn't cheer me up—especially that line about "all the customers" getting sore.

"You know," he went on, "you're playing to pretty stiff competition. Spike Jones is autographing his records this afternoon over in the music department."

I fingered the fountain pen nervously, and we made little jokes about pens that write under water, as was the fashion in those remote times.

Then my customer arrived.

He was a young fellow, maybe twenty, and he hovered near by and watched me for a while. Then he came up and began a studious examination of the books on the table. At last he settled on an anthology which I had committed.

"Tell me something," he said. "What's in this book?"

I tried to tell him.

"I read all the others," he said, "when I was in the service. This one I missed. What I wanna know is what's in it?"

I tried to tell him again.

"Yeh," he said, "but what I really wanna know is do you knock women in this one too?"

"How do you mean, knock women?"

"Well," he said, "you knock women in all the others. Do you knock women in this one?"

I said that I hadn't been aware that I ever knocked women, but I wisely added that if I knocked women in the other books, then I knocked them a bit in this one too. I didn't want to lose him.

Now the young man had a long debate with himself—whether he ought to buy this book or simply go away and forget it all. He asked for more details about its contents. To the best of my ability I began reciting from it. He argued and fussed and fumed, and he looked at it inside and out, and hefted it, and prodded it like a woman buying a head of lettuce, and finally he said with an air of foolhardiness: "I suppose I might as well buy it."

He gave his money to one of the clerks and I felt jubilant. Then he got a chair and, pulling it alongside me, opened the book to the flyleaf and said:

"Now. Before we get down to this signing business, I got a question I want to ask you. Did Betty Hutton actually climb all over you like you said in that book?"

"Yes."

"I don't believe it."

"Well, she did."

He stared at me curiously.

"How'd you get 'er to do it?" he demanded. "How does a fella get her to climb all over you like that?"

"I don't know," I told him. "I was just sitting there, and the next thing I knew she was climbing all over me."

"Right in front of everybody?"

"Yep."

"Keee-rist!" He thought about it for a while, apparently with pleasure, then sighed and returned to the book.

"Now," he said, resuming his businesslike air, "we got to be careful what we write in here. I want you to knock women some more. Write something that's a good knock on women."

We had a fifteen-minute discussion over this point. How

did he want me to knock women? He tried to explain it, but somehow it wasn't quite clear to me. Finally I had a thought.

"Is there," I asked, "any one particular woman you want me to knock?"

"Now you got it!"

"What's her name?"

"Joyce."

"You want me to knock this Joyce?"

"Give it to her good!" he said grimly. "Beat her brains out!"

So I steadied my pen and wrote in that graceful script of mine:

"To Bob—from one who knows that Joyce is an awful stinker. H. Allen Smith."

He examined it and beamed.

"That's the ticket!" he said. "That'll fix 'er!"

Then he got up and put the book under his arm and hurried away. My customer. My fan. I hated to see him go. My watch said five o'clock. I stood up in that awful void and shook hands with the manager and the clerks and drove out to my sister's house and just beat hell out of my nephew Mike in a game of cutthroat croquet.

Chapter 9

William F. Fox, Jr., is the dean of Indiana sports writers, meaning that he has been on the job since the Kickapoo Indians moved into the state from Wisconsin. I well remember that back when I was fumbling out sports copy in Huntington, Mr. Fox was already star performer of the Indianapolis *News* sports pages. In fact, almost all fledgling newspapermen in the state figured that if they could ever reach the eminence achieved by Bill Fox, then this would be the best of all possible Indianas.

Mr. Fox is a friend of the Sullivans, and one evening he and half a dozen other Hoosiers came to the house for several hours of sitting around and chewing the lean. Mr. Fox arrived direct from the Indianapolis Speedway, where qualifications trials were being run. Throughout that week the people of Indianapolis talked of little else but the 500-mile race, this being the occasion of its renewal after a four-year wartime interruption.

There had been a crack-up in the qualification runs that afternoon and a driver had been killed. Mr. Fox was depressed about this, and when he told about it all the other Indianapolis citizens in the room became gloomy and sorrowful. I detected something fundamentally wrong in this wholesale period of mourning for the victim of the crash, but it took me a little while to puzzle it out.

Everyone in Indiana is Speedway-conscious on the thirtieth of each May, and there was even a time when I myself knew what "bore" and "stroke" and "piston displacement" meant. My favorite story about the big race, however, is not an automobile story but a newspaper anecdote.

The editor of a small-town daily paper in Indiana decided one year that he would hold his press until he got the flash announcing the winner of the race. This was before the time of radio sportscasts, and the editor had to depend on a press association to supply him with the big news. He communicated with the press association's correspondent at the track, explaining his needs. After the race had started he began to get nervous, fearing there would be a slip-up, so he wired the correspondent at the track reminding him that his afternoon edition was being held for the flash.

The correspondent, just to reassure the editor that he was on his toes, sent back a wire which said, "Will overhead winner." This means, if you didn't know it, that he would flash the name of the winner by telegram. The newspaper editor, however, was in such a state of nervous tension that he misinterpreted the message. There was a great whooping and hollering in his shop and he went to press. His page-one banner line read:

WILL OVERHEAD WINS RACE

And under that a brief bulletin announcing that a dark horse, Will Overhead, driving at terrific speed, had flashed across the finish line to capture the 500-mile classic.

I had been to the race before. Back in 1925 I was working for a newspaper in Louisville, and on the strength of my being a part-time Hoosier I was given press credentials and sent to the race with instructions to write some pieces about the crowds and about the Ku Klux Klan parade that was being held on the eve of the race.

My memory of that assignment is clouded, save for one incident. During the long and, to me, boring hours when the cars were screaming around the track I wandered onto the lawn in front of the press pagoda. I went down to the fence next to the track and stood there watching the racers shoot past and trying to figure out something I could write about.

Suddenly somebody spoke to me. "How do you like the Miller Specials?" the voice said. I turned and found an old geezer standing next to me, wearing an overcoat and an old felt hat. I say he was an old geezer because, being around eighteen at the time, I considered anybody past thirty to be an old geezer and I had no use for old geezers, having not yet achieved geezerhood myself. I didn't answer him, except to shrug my shoulders in a manner that said I wished he'd go away. But he continued talking about the weather, and the crowd, and the drivers, and finally I just turned around and walked away. Gabby old honyock, I thought. Probably chiseled his way into the press section. I went back to the pagoda and immediately was surrounded by other newspapermen, all of them demanding to know what I had got out of Henry Ford. Some of them had approached Ford earlier, but he had told them he had nothing to say. They had seen me down by the fence, ostensibly carrying on a long and intimate conversation with Henry, and since there was an agreement that all news was to be shared, they insisted that I give them the information I had got from Ford. I tried to tell them that I hadn't known it was Ford and that I had shut my ears against his gabble and couldn't remember a thing he said. Think they'd believe me? Not a bit. I was ostracized by the gentlemen of the press for the remainder of the day—ostracized and called foul names.

Thus it was that I had had a little experience in connection with the 500-mile race, and as William F. Fox, Jr., and the others in the Sullivan living room were heaving sorrowful sighs over the afternoon accident, I seemed to sense that the whole picture was wrong. As I remembered it, people *wanted* to see crashes at the Speedway. They *wanted* to see other people killed. Well, maybe things had changed, so I kept my mouth shut. But between the time of that gathering and the time of the race I found out that some people, at least, were of the old school. The next day, in fact, I stopped in front of an office building on Meridian Street just north of the Circle. In the window was a huge diagram of the Speedway, grandstands and all. I was trying to locate the section where we had seats when a man came up beside me (not Henry Ford). He was a respectable citizen, or at least he

looked like a respectable citizen, being well costumed, having a pinkish face with an assortment of jowls, and speaking with the twang of authority and self-possession. He looked to be the typical American business executive of fable, and for that reason I suspect that he was very likely a dope peddler or a free-lance plumber or an author of realistic novels. In the pleasant fashion of the Midwest, he started talking to me. He pointed to a section of the Speedway grandstands as indicated on the chart and said:

"There's the spot. Right smack on that little old curve, right there. That's the place to watch it. Look at this." He took out a wallet and removed two tickets from it and showed them to me. Again he pointed to the chart. "That's where *I'll* be. That's where I sit every year. You wanna see 'em get killed, that's the spot. Man, they really get it on that curve!"

I didn't, to be sure, find anyone who came right out and said they hoped somebody got killed, but I found ample evidence that most spectators at the Speedway attend the race for the thrill of seeing a car hit a concrete wall, or another car, or two other cars, or—better yet—leave the track, hurtle through the air, and land on a group of customers.

The Torrid Zone shifted its position and overlapped Indianapolis on the day of the race. The Indianapolis newspapers said that it was the biggest crowd ever to attend a sporting event in the history of the world. I'll concede it, and I'll also say that another record was established—it was the greasiest sporting event in all history.

The race begins at ten o'clock in the morning, after a lot of bombs have been shot off, and continues for something over four hours. Tradition dictates that fried chicken shall be eaten when the race is about half finished. Almost everyone fetches a hamper of fried chicken, and when the sun gets over the yardarm the customers in the stands remove their attention from the track and go to work on the vittles. This is a sight worth seeing—tens of thousands of men, women, and children gnawing away at fried chicken while funny-looking little vehicles, called by such names as Spike Jones Special and LGS Spring Clutch Special and Noc-Out Hose Clamp Special, roar past them at speeds considerably in excess of a hundred miles an hour. Viewing this prospect, I had a feeling that every fryable chicken in Indiana had been slaughtered for the occasion.

There is purpose behind the 500-mile race over and above the making of money from the sale of admission tickets. At least they say that the race serves as a sort of laboratory in which automobile manufacturers learn how to improve their product. As I sat there ankle-deep in chicken bones, however, I couldn't figure how the race was of any immediate benefit to the ordinary motorist.

As an automobile driver I found little drama in the fact that one ball bearing was standing up better than another ball bearing. That race ought to be dressed up somehow so that it will have greater significance to the nation's motorists—to people like myself who refer to a distributor as a thingumajig. I had a few ideas, and if Bill Fox wants to start crusading for them, he's welcome to do it.

The putting on and taking off of chains in winter, for example, is the major curse of owning an automobile. One of the best editorials I ever read appeared a couple of years ago in the North Westchester *Times*, a weekly. It was brief and to the point. It praised the automotive industry for the marvelous mechanical advancements it has made, for year-by-year technical improvements, and for advances in styling (recently I bought a car that gets out and washes its own windshield). However, said the *Times*, the automotive industry has never done anything about the skid-chain nuisance. A motorist has to get out and wallow in the snow and grovel in the mud, and cuss and freeze his fingers, just as he did in the time of Theodore Dreiser's Hoosier hegira. This is a subject that touches me deeply because I live in the country where the wind blows and the snow piles high on the roads and driveways. When the man on the radio says intermittent drizzle for New York City, that means blizzard where I live. I don't mind the hours and hours of shoveling; it's those damn chains that kill me. I can wear out a set of chains without ever leaving my property, simply trying to get them on the tires.

It would be an intelligent innovation, therefore, if the Speedway racers be required to stop occasionally in front of the stands, put on chains, drive a lap or so, stop again and take off chains. Better yet, put the top executives of General Motors and Ford and Chrysler and the other manufacturers in overalls and compel *them* to put on and take off chains. Maybe they'd figure something out for us.

Another thing. All the rule books about driving tell us that when your car starts to skid, you are to turn the wheels in the direction in which you are skidding. Now I do my share of skidding and I try to remember that rule, but only once in my life have I ever obeyed it. The Sawmill River Parkway was icy and I was concentrating on the probability of a skid when it came. I started skidding to the right. I turned my front wheels to the right, fighting off an instinctive urge to turn them the other way. I went through a snowbank, missed a concrete culvert by half a foot, and was heading briskly for a tree when the snow stopped me. It took a tractor to get me out of there. I've checked with other drivers of my acquaintance and I've found two or three who *claim* they always turn the wheels according to the prescribed rules. Only one of these, I think, is telling the truth. He is a man who handles the tiller on the rear end of a hook-and-ladder truck, and if he didn't turn his wheels in the proper direction, there would be ladder rungs scattered from hell to breakfast.

There must be some merit to the rule. Perhaps if you were out in the middle of a large field, a proving ground, and started to skid, the clever thing to do would be to turn the wheels in the direction of the skid. On most roads, however, there are boundaries lined with poles and trees and culverts and ditches and stone walls. Perhaps Mr. Fox can arrange to have a stretch of the Speedway track, in front of the stands, covered with a sheet of ice so the drivers can go into skids and demonstrate the proper method of turning the wheels in the direction of the skid. If he does arrange it, I assure you I don't want to be in the neighborhood.

I have all sorts of ideas about how to improve the lot of the ordinary motorist, including a scheme to do away with the well-known highway menace, the moron driver, i.e., woman. I don't think I'd better discuss it here.

One of the reasons I enjoy driving a car is that it gives me a chance to get the hate out of my system. Hate-on-the-highway is an institution occupying a high place in our modern civilization. To me it is a very peculiar human institution. The godawful glares that drivers exchange as they pass each other, the mutual hatred between motorist and pedestrian, these manifestations seem to constitute the ultimate in righteous wrath. Take a group of motorists assembled in a tourist camp. They fraternize, talk affably of their experiences on the road, exchange addresses, buy beer for each other, lend one another Lux or liver pills, and sometimes they even put their heads together and sing. Let those same people meet on the open highway and hatred for each other occupies their hearts and they scream curses at each other.

I have a brother named Sam who has his eccentric moments when he's at the wheel of his car. He is not much bigger than a jockey and he has an ungovernable temper plus more courage than befits a lad of his size. He is one of those drivers who scream at other drivers. He has a fine command of unconventional English and he doesn't care how many large, tough men are occupying the car which offends him; if he considers that they have been driving stupidly, and he usually does, he leans out the window and shrieks bad words at them. You know the type. It is inevitable that now and then one of his targets is going to take serious offense. He is going to slap his foot on the brake and stop his car or truck and get out and approach Sam with intent to kill. But Sam is a wise one. He drives with a hatchet on the front seat beside him. As the wrathful victim of his curses comes charging down on his car, Sam sits placidly behind the wheel, reaches down and picks up the hatchet, and draws it back like an Indian preparing to split a paleskull. Then, as the enemy comes within range and makes ready to clout Sam or reach in and grab him and drag him through the window and beat him to death, Sam says through his teeth: "Lay a hand on me, you son-of-a-bitch, and your arm comes off at the elbow!" Thus far he has escaped without bruise or blemish, but I have a standing order at a florist shop for a nice wreath. After all, he's my brother.

But let us now say farewell to the Indianapolis Speedway. Who knows what new joys are glimmering in the distance? Let us be off, down the broad highway, past the lovely fields where the lupines grow just like in Steinbeck's book about the bus.

We stopped for a couple of days in Indiana's oldest town, Vincennes, on the banks of the Wabash. I was tempted to go by way of Terre Haute, where Dreiser's birthplace is still standing. I felt almost certain that I could stand in front of that little house and feel depressed. Lord knows I hadn't done so well on my own hook thus far. But then I got to thinking how Dreiser sometimes used bad grammar and, being a purist myself, I decided the hell with it and headed for Vincennes.

This is an interesting town if you go for old things. For example, the Cathedral Library has the oldest book in Indiana. I didn't get the name of it—that doesn't seem important. There are statues and monuments and markers all over the place, plus the magnificent George Rogers Clark Memorial which stands on the banks of the Wabash. This is a high, white, round affair encircled by massive Doric columns (I got that out of a book; I wouldn't personally know a Doric column from a laughing willow). I walked over from the hotel to the memorial, pausing along the way to have a good look at the Wabash, sniffed the air for a breath of new-mown hay and didn't smell any, or if I did I didn't recognize it as such, and would have looked through the sycamores for some gleaming candlelight except that I'm not acquainted with the build of a sycamore and anyway it was daytime.

Within the memorial I found a man who has the job of showing off the place to the multitudes of tourists who pass through Vincennes. You couldn't properly call this man a guide because there is only one high circular room in the memorial; as well have a guide in a silo. He is more on the order of a lecturer, and he is so good that I went back two times in two days to hear him again, and when I finished my business farther west and headed for home I deliberately returned by way of Vincennes so I could hear him a couple more times.

He was a thickset man around forty with a permanent look of wide-eyed wonder in his eyes, a sort of startled expression, as though he simply couldn't believe that he had grown up to occupy such an eminent and enviable position. I don't mean to say that he was in any way overbearing; the exact opposite was true.

On the walls of the circular room are seven tall murals done by Ezra Winter of New York and depicting the exploits of George Rogers Clark and other matters connected with the opening of the West. The main job of our friend, Wide-eyes, is to conduct tourist parties around the room and recite out the significance of these murals. He does it in a set speech, delivered in as pure a Hoosier dialect as I have ever heard, and he never deviates by as much as a single word. I got the impression that the recital has become so routine with him that he goes through it without consciousness of what he is saying. I thought of engaging a stenographer to make the circuit with him and take down his lecture word for word, but then I figured that the presence of a stenographer might upset him and throw him off his stride.

On one of my four times around with him a circumstance arose which put him in a panic and brought out of him the only display of emotion he ever showed in my presence. The thing took me back a number of years, to the time I was working with Walter O'Keefe, trying to write a radio script that would capture the fancy of a cigarette manufacturer. You may remember that Mr. O'Keefe is good at mimicking the *March of Time* man who avers that time marches on in a tone that suggests an atom bomb is about to explode in his pants. In the script we included an episode in which Mr. O'Keefe, as the *March of Time* announcer, was making a tour through the great parent plant of the American Putty Knife Corporation.

"From the assembly line," boomed the voice, "the putty knives go through the counting process. We now approach the door which opens into the counting division where men trained over a lifetime, passing their unique skill from one generation to another, make an accurate tally of the day's production."

(*Sound of door opening.*)

VOICE I: Nine hundred and ninety-nine thousand, nine hundred and ninety-six; nine hundred and ninety-nine thousand, nine hundred and ninety-seven; nine hundred and ninety-nine thous——

VOICE II: Hey, Joe, what time is it?

VOICE I: Twenty after two. (*Pause.*) One, two, three, four, five . . .

The lecturer in the Clark Memorial was working that

warm day in his shirt sleeves. A bum expression. Sounds as if the main part of his shirt had been ripped off his back, and front, and only the sleeves were left. Actually he was working with a complete shirt on and no coat. Half a dozen tourists, including myself, were hearing the epic story of George Rogers Clark and his men, made even epicker by the peculiar enunciation of the lecturer.

Standing next to me was a lean, weather-beaten man in a Sunday suit. He attracted my attention because of his nervously eager manner. He couldn't hold still, and quite obviously he wasn't paying too much attention to the lecture. He acted like a dumb child who has to go to the bathroom and hasn't got enough sense to go without being told. He squirmed and twitched, and I noticed that he kept glancing across the room toward Number Six in the series of murals, the one called Marietta—The Northwest a New Territory.

The information contained in the lecture is artfully contrived. It is assumed that a majority of the people who visit the memorial are Midwesterners, and due recognition is taken of the fact that a Midwesterner likes to have his facts solid and substantial. The romantic aspects of Clark's achievement are all right, but I noticed that most of the tourists really didn't perk up until the lecturer got down to brass tacks—the exact weight of the stone that went into the memorial; the cost of the land and the tonnage of the buildings that had to be knocked down to make room for the memorial; the number of pounds of paint used by Ezra Winter; the height of the ceiling in the New York studio where Ezra Winter did the murals. The lecturer, incidentally, always refers to the muralist as "Ezry Winters."

My neighbor, the lean man, grew more jittery by the minute, and I could tell that some sort of crisis was approaching for him. At last the lecturer finished with the mural about the surrender of Fort Sackville. He took a few steps to the right, getting in position for the next—Marietta.

"Marietta——" began the lecturer.

"MARIETTA!" cried the lean man. "Man, that's whirr I come from! You want some hist'ry! Goadamighty I'll give you some hist'ry!"

Wide-eyes turned and looked at the man from Marietta.

He swallowed a few times and blinked his eyes. He wasn't angry at the interruption, he was hurt, wounded. The man from Marietta was all but shouting now. Phooey on Vincennes and George Rogers Clark and Fort Sackville and Cahokia and all the rest—he was from Marietta and if anybody wanted any *real* hist'ry, 'y god that's where they had it, Marietta.

I don't think I ever felt so sorry for anyone in my life as I did for Wide-eyes. He had the look of a spaniel that has just been flogged. Not only had this interloper challenged the sacred story of Old Vincennes; he had done the same thing to our lecturer that had been done to the tabulator of putty knives. Wide-eyes looked around the room as though seeking help, but none was forthcoming. At last he turned and herded us, all but Mr. Marietta, across the room to Mural Number One, and then in a voice that trembled he began, "Here we see George Rogers Clark entering Kentucky . . ." He was starting all over again, and he didn't reach his full stride until he saw that the man from Marietta was leaving the room. When he got back to the Marietta mural I could detect only the faintest suggestion of scorn in his voice, and after we had finished with the murals he took us back and showed us the figure of a turkey in the French marble of the wainscot. "This figure of the turkey," he said, "was first discovered by a little child from Tleedo, Ohiuh. It looks just like a turkey." And it did, too.

The period in which we were traveling through the Midwest was an unhealthy one, economically. Those were the times, you might say, that tried men's souls. To get a hotel room it was necessary to telephone ahead a week or two before you wanted the accommodations. Meat was still hard to get. It was the era of the nylon lines and all the other lines. I remember walking up Main Street in Vincennes, preoccupied with trying to get a word out of my head. I get words running through my mind as some people get songs. Usufruct. That word had popped into my head and I couldn't get rid of the scamp. I think it is an interesting word, and for a long time I had wanted to use it and had been waiting for an opportunity to work it into a composition.

Usufruct, as a noun, means: "The right of using and enjoying the fruits or profits of an estate or other thing belonging to another, without impairing the substance." I've never personally been in a situation like that. Whenever I enjoy the fruits or profits of an estate or other thing belonging to another, you can depend on me to impair the substance. Usufruct is also a verb, meaning to hold property subject to usufruct. It is difficult for me to use it in a sentence; it doesn't sound right to say, for example, "Charlie was usufructed at Camden last week."

My mind was going "usufruct, usufruct, usufruct" to the measure of my footsteps up Main Street when I saw a sight that was common all over the United States early in the year 1946. Seemingly appearing from nowhere, half a dozen people formed the beginning of a line in front of a store, and before I had taken another ten steps the line was half a block long. Nylons, I thought. Or maybe even better than that, pork chops, or cold chisels, or pipe cleaners, or wall-to-wall carpeting. As was the custom, I stepped into the line and moved slowly along with it. I rather hoped it would be nylons, my wife being urgently in need of hosiery. By the time I had reached the entrance to the store the line behind me extended half a block to the corner, then disappeared around that corner, and very likely was snaked out as far as the Wabash. On reaching the doorway I was able to see inside, and when I saw what was being sold I stepped out of the line and resumed usufructing. It was chewing gum, and I don't use it.

We are now ready to cross the Lincoln Memorial Bridge into Illinois. The bridge got its name from the fact that Abraham Lincoln and his folks crossed the Wabash at this point to settle near Decatur, Illinois. Before we enter Illinois, however, I must consider the fact that you might possibly still be interested in Indiana. I've collected a few items of interest—things you might want to know about in case you ever go touring among the Hoosiers.

My friends in Peoria, Illinois, may be shocked to learn that Indiana has a Peoria. Some pioneers from the East were mushing toward Illinois intending to settle in Peoria, Illinois. They came to a spot in the Mississinewa Valley (Mississinewa means Mississippi with its back end screwed up) where they decided the scenery was so nice that they'd settle there instead, and they called their village Peoria.

If you should come upon the little town of Oxford, that's where Dan Patch, celebrated harness racer, was foaled on a manure pile in 1896. I include this item for the benefit of literary critics, who might wish to draw a parallel between Dan Patch and myself.

In the basement of the Johnson County courthouse is a little museum. One of the exhibits is a ladies' fan, spotted with the blood of Abraham Lincoln. The fan belonged to a woman who claimed she was sitting in the theater box with the Lincolns on the night of the assassination and that's how the blood got on it. I'd just as soon not see it.

In Indianapolis I met a woman who said that she believes sex "is a sacred thing." Lawks!

If you are a humorist or a radio comedian who enjoys using the word "Kokomo" in an attempt to get a laugh, it should be of interest to you to know that the town, by rights, should be called Kokomoko. Kokomoko was the Indian chief for whom the town was named.

The town of Rockfield is small but famous, being the birthplace of a boar named Evolution. Someone with a fine opinion of hogs once paid $25,000 for Evolution. Any time a hog brings in $25,000, I consider him a great credit to his race; he is hogdom's answer to the many Hoosier authors who have, at one time or another, invented characters who called other characters, "You swine!" I wonder what the owner of a $25,000 hog would feed the creature. Probably slops him with chocolate malteds.

If you are musically inclined and ever go through Elkhart, you'll want to know about Captain Conn. He came home to Elkhart after the Civil War between the States for Southern Independence and opened a little grocery store. Evenings he played cornet in the town band. One day he got in a fight with another man and came out of it with a badly bruised lip. In order to continue playing the cornet with the town band, Captain Conn devised a soft rubber mouthpiece for his horn. Apparently Elkhart was a great town for fist fights in those days and bruised lips were commonplace, because Captain Conn was soon flooded with orders from other horn players who wanted rubber mouthpieces. He made a lathe out of an old sewing machine and started turning them out in his spare time. Thus the origin of the great band-instrument house of Conn.

The celebrated town of Santa Claus was platted in 1846. The platters named it Sante Fe. When they got a postmaster, he told them there was already a Sante Fe in Indiana and they'd have to change it. "Oh," said the settlers, "you are nothing but old nuts. If we cain't call it Sante *Fe,* how would you like it if we called it Sante *Claus?*" Be-danged if it didn't stick.

Near Terre Haute is a town called Hymera. When first settled it was called Pittsburg, but, just as happened at Santa Claus, there was already a Pittsburg in Indiana. The postmaster was given the task of finding a substitute name. He had a tall daughter named Mary. He called the town High Mary in her honor, but eventually the name was corrupted to its present form. Still another town with a lyrical name is Gnaw Bone. When this place was first settled one of the inhabitants was asked the whereabouts of another inhabitant, whose wife probably wanted him. "I seed him," said this early Hoosier, "a-settin' on a log above the sawmill a-gnawin' on a bone." This seems to me to be a poor excuse for naming a town, but the books say that's how Gnaw Bone got its name. Some people considered the name offensive and lacking in dignity, and a few years ago the Indiana Highway Commission changed it to West Point. The local gentry, however, continued to call it Gnaw Bone and so did the people for miles around, and in the end the

Highway Commission had to yield, and the official name of the town is once again Gnaw Bone.

Now let the sun come up from the corrupt East and flood the fructiferous usufructs of Illinois; let the golden rays shimmer on the ribbon of Highway 50 and spangle the gooseberries in the fen. The little lad of McLeansboro is at last coming home; that carefree, happy, laughing, non-taxpaying tyke of Decatur is crossing the Wabash! Honor him, Illinois! Salute him, you Suckers! And don't call him vulgar, for if you do he will, like Esar-Haddon the Assyrian, lay waste to all of Egypt!

Chapter 10

We entered the state of my nativity and rambled around in it at some length under a severe handicap: we had no *Illinois Guide*. Such a book had been put together and published in 1939 but it had gone out of print during the war. The original edition must have been a small one, because I couldn't locate a copy of it before starting on the trip. I advertised for it, with no success, and noticed at the time that a lot of other people were advertising for it. I wanted it particularly for the basic information it would give me about the town and the county in which I was born. So I decided I would try for it in bookstores along the way.

In the larger cities I visited or telephoned all the bookstores but always got the same answer: the *Illinois Guide* had become as rare as my first novel. And in the lesser cities I found that books were things that are either rented or found at the public library. There were places calling themselves bookstores, but they were loaded with greeting cards and penwipers and dolls that holler mama while wetting themselves. When I asked for the *Illinois Guide* in these places they always tried to sell me road maps of Illinois. I had a long controversy with a lady in such a place at Vincennes. She got out a fancy road map and I said no, that wasn't what I wanted.

"But," she said, "this happens to be an Illinois guide."

"Yes, I know. But what I'm after is a book——"

"Look," she insisted, opening pages of the map, "this is a book. I don't get what you're driving at."

Choosing my words with care, I made an effort to explain to her how each state in the Union had a guide—a big fat book with a hard cover on it. She had never heard of them. Moreover, she indicated that she didn't believe me, and when I refused to buy the road map she suggested that I was mighty hard to please, and she seemed happy when I left her store. She was not alone—I had similar experiences in similar stores. And as for the public libraries, I tried several of them and found that they were either closed or, when open, the librarians hadn't heard of any such books; and where they had heard of them, they hadn't bothered about getting copies.

There are somewhere between fifty and a hundred of these books, counting all the states and those devoted to the major cities of the country, plus a few concerned with specific highway routes. They were, in every case, produced by the government and paid for by the government. I don't know what system was used in parceling them out to various book publishers, but it was clearly a mistake. I wish there were some way in which the government could now step in and drag all of them back and bring them under a single authority so that they could be revised and kept in print and brought up to date every few years. Goddammit, as my father used to say, what we need is a little *system* around here!

So we rode into Illinois without benefit of a guide, not even knowing that the highway we traveled was the route of the old Trace Road which was originally marked out by herds of buffalo galloping westward, like dopes, to keep an appointment with destiny in the person of Buffalo Bill; and after the buffalo the Indians had used it, and after the Indians the pony-express riders—called postriders in these parts but performing the same functions as the pony express. We crossed the Embarras River with no idea of how it got its name, though we speculated about it, and I had the mistaken theory that the name originated from the condition in which some pioneer swimmer entered its waters.

As you may already have guessed, I have an abnormal

interest in the origin of place names. Twenty-odd years ago another boy and I were roaming through Texas and Arkansas trying to work an advertising racket. In the latter state we were approaching the town of Smackover and we got into a discussion of how the name originated. My theory was that a couple of the early settlers had got into an argument and one had flattened the other—smacked him over. I've forgotten what my friend contended, but his guess was as

wrong as mine. When we reached Smackover we went to a drugstore and cornered the proprietor and asked him for the answer. After telling us we were both wrong, he gave us the story. The first settlers, he said, arrived by muleback, and in order to reach the site of their settlement they had to ford a deep stream. The first mule to start across had no more than got into the stream when the water "went smack over his head." That, said the druggist, was the true version. For twenty years I've been satisfied with his explanation, but now I've looked the thing up. One book says that the French called the place Chemin Couvert, "covered road," which in time was corrupted to Smackover. Another book says early French hunters found dense thickets of sumac in the neighborhood and called it *Sumac-couvert*, which in time became Smackover. Who is to be believed? Personally I'm sticking with the druggist and his mule.

For lack of the *Illinois Guide*, I drove past the birthplace of William Jennings Bryan without giving it a glance. Had I known about it I would have given it a glance. In recent years I have come to have a certain admiration for Bryan, based on a single incident. He was campaigning somewhere in the Midwest and his train stopped at a hamlet where a crowd of farmers had congregated to hear him orate. Bryan got off the train and looked around for a platform, but nobody had put one up and his eye fell on an old manure-spreader standing near the tracks. Without hesitation Bryan climbed upon this vehicle, faced his audience, and opened his oration with: "This is the first time I have ever delivered a speech while standing on the Republican platform."

The center of population of the United States is now in Illinois, though the Census Bureau has not yet got around to nailing it down in a specific place. Very likely it is somewhere in the neighborhood of the point where we entered the state, and for all I know, we may have run over it and killed it. It moved across the Wabash from Indiana sometime after 1940, probably in the dead of night, otherwise the Hoosiers would have figured out some way of keeping it on their side of the river. It has been in Indiana for many years, and Indiana has been proud and boastful about having it there. They wouldn't let it get over into Illinois without a battle. The history of Indiana is filled with stories of kidnaped colleges and stolen county seats. When those Hoosiers want a thing they go get it. I imagine the center of population escaped to Illinois unnoticed; had the Hoosiers been alert they'd have taken steps to prevent it. The only way I can figure it could be done would entail a lot of work and fist-fighting. Everybody in Indiana would have to go out to southern California and seize several million citizens and drag them back and tie them to trees somewhere east of

Illinois and keep them tied up until the next census. They still have two years before the next census, if they want to do it. Meanwhile the center of population is across the river and slowly inching westward, probably through a swamp, and Illinois is already beginning to take pride in its presence.

The people of Illinois are known to the rest of the country as Suckers, and their land is the Sucker State. They don't particularly like the name and shy away from it, preferring to call their domain the Prairie State.

First and foremost I am an Egyptian, or former Egyptian, but at the same time I am a Sucker, or former Sucker, and I have no objection to being called one. The name doesn't indicate that a citizen of Illinois is an easy mark, never to be given an even break. You won't find any Illinois people grouped in front of the pitchmen who sell miraculous potato peelers in Times Square. In fact, as I write these words there is a man out in Illinois busy making "genuine Indian arrowheads" which he sells at fancy prices and which are so cleverly fashioned that the foremost authorities on genuine Indian arrowheads have been fooled by them.

Also in Illinois there was once a man who put an ad in country weeklies thoroughout the state, saying:

Sure way to kill potato bugs: send twenty two-cent stamps for a recipe that cannot fail.

He had to hire a dray to handle the mail that came in, and inside of two weeks more than seven thousand Illinois farmers had sent in their stamps. After a while, when the farmers got no response, a group of them armed themselves with heavy clubs and went to the address mentioned in the ad. They were told at the office that the potato-bug man had been called to Europe on business and that all he had left behind was a package containing several thousand slips of paper on which were printed:

Put your bug on a shingle. Then hit it with another shingle.

Few citizens of Illinois, I imagine, know the origin of the nickname Sucker. The likeliest explanation may be found in *A Treasury of American Folklore,* in the form of a letter written from Illinois to the Providence *Journal* many years ago. Here it is:

The Western prairies are, in many places, full of holes made by the "crawfish" (a fresh-water shellfish similar in form to the lobster) which descends to the water beneath. In early times, when travelers wended their way over these immense plains, they very prudently provided themselves with a long hollow weed, and when thirsty, thrust it into these natural artesians, and thus easily supplied their longings. The crawfish-well generally contains pure water, and the manner in which the traveler drew forth the refreshing element gave him the name of "Sucker."

If the people of Illinois still shy away from their time-honored nickname, let them look westward and take satisfaction in the knowledge that their next-door neighbors, the Missourians, are called Pukes.

There is some dispute about why the southern part of Illinois is called Egypt. Some authorities say the name came from the valley of the Kaskaskia, which was likened to the valley of the Nile by its first white settlers. Others contend that the name had its origin at the confluence of the Ohio and the Mississippi, where Cairo stands. Cairo is a big town (pronounced like canned syrup), but there is also a Thebes in the region, and a Delta, and there used to be a Goshen. Carmi, a neighbor of McLeansboro, took its name from one of the sons of Jacob who migrated to Egypt.

The *Egyptian Key* takes violent exception when anyone refers to the section as "Little" Egypt. This sterling publication says: "The area is not small geographically, industrially, nor intellectually . . . Egypt is here to be a mighty force in Illinois. It is not little."

The magazine, as well as the people of the region, takes pride in the name. As soon as we had driven down as far as Mount Vernon we began seeing signs: Egyptian Taxicab Company. Egyptian Pharmacy. Egyptian Bottling Works. Things like that. And in some localities, I understand, there has been an attempt to copy the basic features of Egyptian architecture, though I didn't see any of these buildings. I

126

think it would be nice to have a county jail in the form of a pyramid. You wouldn't have to tie bed sheets together in order to escape from it. Just saw the bars, climb out the window, and slide.

At this point I could sketch out for you all that is known about Egyptian architecture, but it would be full of masta-bas, propylons, clerestory, torus molding, batter, cavetto cornices, Osiride pillars from Medinet Habu, and you wouldn't be able to understand it unless you were an architect—I mean an Egyptian architect 3,947 years of age. The temptation is strong to do it because there is need for a more scholarly approach in this manuscript.

Years ago when I was employed on the Denver *Post* there came a period when that newspaper hired a literary editor. I pestered her from dawn to dusk pleading for the honor of writing some book reviews. Finally she gave me a volume, a war book, and I reviewed it. I said that it was the greatest war book ever written, not excluding *The Red Badge of Courage*. Miss Bancroft toned my review down a bit, but I think she was impressed by my reference to *The Red Badge of Courage*, which suggested that I had been around in the world of literature; the fact is I had never read it, but had only heard about it. The second book she gave me was a collection of short stories, and in my review I said that this was the greatest book of short stories ever published. She spoke to me gently after that one, suggesting that I get control of myself, and tried me once again with a travel book called *The Desert Road to Turkestan*. This book, I wrote, was far and away the finest travel book ever put together by mortal man. I turned the review in and Miss Bancroft struck me off her list. The fact remains that I have read a good many travel books and know something about the technique employed in writing them. A man can't just go traveling around, looking at things, and then sit down and write about what he saw. Now and then he must show signs of scholarship, if not wisdom.

At this point in my narrative, therefore, I see an opportunity for a serious job of scholarly research. We are visiting Egypt in Illinois and there is a larger and more complex Egypt across the water. From a cultural point of view is there any similarity between the peoples of the two Egypts? Yes. And if you will kindly hold still, I shall undertake to elucidate some of those cultural parallels.

For example, henna is grown so extensively in Egypt that . . . Just a moment. I have reference here to the Egypt over yonder, not the Illinois Egypt. Perhaps we should try to keep it clear just which Egypt we are discussing. Under the circumstances, I imagine the *Egyptian Key* will permit me to call the Egypt of the old country "Big Egypt" and the Illinois product "Little Egypt." The Arabic name for Big Egypt is El Qutr el Masri. I could use that, but if I did I'd have to get some matching name for Little Egypt. I could refer to Little Egypt as Let-Us-Quit-This-Misery. I believe that the *Egyptian Key* would prefer that I say "Little Egypt." So be it.

Henna is grown so extensively in Big Egypt that all henna is generally called Egyptian henna. The Big Egyptian women do not use henna on their hair, but paint the palms of their hands and the soles of their feet with it. The men henna the tails of their horses. None of this foolishness is practiced in Little Egypt.

In the old days they had many priestesses in Big Egypt, and it was the duty of such a lady to shake her sistrum.

Among the great men of Old Big Egypt was a ruler named Ptolemy Philadelphus, who was the son of Ptolemy Pretty Maiden. The latter part of the foregoing sentence is a sort of joke. I think I made it up, but I have a vague notion that somebody else invented it. If so, the original author may have it back, postpaid. Now, this Ptolemy Philadelphus developed the tremendous Museum and Library at Alexandria. In it were 532,000 books. They were not books as we know them, but rolls similar to those used on a player piano. They were made of a tough substance called papyrus, and it was much easier in those days for an author to take a copy of his book and go down and beat a critic to death with it. I have had no firsthand experience with this type of book, but I imagine that it was difficult to read one of them in bed; I have a mental picture of Harry Hansen hopelessly snarled in a mile and a half of *Forever Amber*.

The people of Big Egypt were progressive, and in time the

shaduf was replaced by the noria. Some people, of course, didn't like the change.

The pig was sacred in Big Egypt, although if you touched one by accident it was required that you go to the nearest river and walk into it with your clothes on.

Big Egyptians often hit each other with axes.

Antique chairs in Big Egypt usually had legs made in the form of goose heads.

The language of Big Egypt is quite technical, and difficult to understand. The grammar is pure murder. I would explain it for you except that the matter has already been handled quite capably by H. Zimmern in his restrained and limpid work, *Vergleichende Grammatik d. semitischen Sprachen.* H. Zimmern writes like an angel.

A Big Egyptian woman can get a divorce from her husband. Suppose, then, she decides she really loves him after all and wants to remarry him. It is necessary that she marry and divorce another man (fellah) before she can go back to Number One. So it is that in Big Egypt they have a class of men who are usually old and ugly and blind, and they serve as middlemen in the transaction. The woman in the case simply marries the decrepit one, walks over to another office, divorces him, and then remarries her original soul mate.

Among the peculiarities of the Big Egyptians is the fact that they like to eat mutton. For this reason they grow tremendous herds of muttons, known in this country as sheep. It is of interest to me that most of their sheep are black. In other words, in Big Egypt if you turn out to be a stinkpot, people very likely will say of you, "Oh, him! He's the white sheep of the family." This expression may in time become common in our own country. In the past we have always said, "He's the black sheep of the family," presupposing that there could be only *one* such in each family. We know this to be fallacious. It is possible—and I speak with scientific authority—for a single family to have more than one heel in its membership. It is even possible to have a family in which everybody is a heel. Usually, however, when a family appears to be composed entirely of black sheep, one of its members turns out to be good. Of him we would say, "He's the white sheep of the family." I'd better get away from this thing—I'm beginning to sound like a column by Henry McLemore.

Now that we have looked into the mores of the other Egypt, let us return to Illinois. Down through the years southern Illinois has been contemptuous of northern Illinois, and for good reason. Egypt was settled and (some say) civilized long before there was any suggestion of a settlement in northern Illinois. The first settlers, in fact, arrived by way of the Wilderness Road and the Ohio River and settled. Almost all of them were Southerners and remain so, in their talk and their customs, to this day. In other words, having been born in Egypt, I am, to all intents and purposes, a sho-nuffer.

I have read that the first settlers of southern Illinois were of Celtic and Anglo-Saxon strain; after a while a few fools from the East got into northern Illinois and tried to establish a civilization up there. Some of these misguided people got up a fort on Lake Michigan and called it Fort Dearborn. In order to do this it was necessary that they get the Indians so drunk they wouldn't know a scalp from a breechclout, and then they decided it was about time they started a town called Chicago.

Now here comes a thing which causes me and every other native Egyptian to swell with pride. Those people up north got themselves a village started, but something was wrong with it—they couldn't attract industry, the river seemed to be running in the wrong direction, and they didn't have a single keg of nails for building a Haymarket to have a riot in. Enviously they looked to the south where, on the banks of the Ohio, stood the thriving little city of Shawneetown. Maybe, said the Northerners, they could get some help from the Egyptians in Shawneetown. A committee was appointed, and its members rode horseback more than three hundred miles and, arriving in Shawneetown, went to the local bank. They described their attempts to make a town on the shore of Lake Michigan and the hardships they were encountering, and said they would like to borrow some money to tide them over. The Shawneetown bankers were dubious about the whole thing, but promised to investigate, and they did. They sent a shrewd Egyptian up to have a look at the village, and when he came back he shook his head from side to side. "Nawp," he said. "It's too fur from Shawneetown to ever amount to nothin'." This was known as the Dred Scott decision.

The fact that the Shawneetown investigator was in error and that Chicago got along without Egyptian aid cannot be attributed to any progressiveness on the part of the early Chicagoans. The whole thing came about by accident, and the accident was a thing called the Erie Canal. This canal proved a great boon to Walter D. Edmonds, providing him with background material for his novels, but it was the blow that broke the prestige of Egypt. As soon as it was completed, great tides of immigrants began moving upon northern Illinois. They came in swarms, and the next thing anybody knew, they had a big Chicago and the fire and the riot and the *Tribune*. Back in once-dominant Egypt they tried to make the best of a bad break. They scoffed and pointed out that *they*, the Egyptians, were Celtic and Anglo-Saxon, whereas northern Illinois was populated by *immigrants*. This argument lacks relevance. Personally, I'd just as soon they had all been Indians.

But let us concern ourselves no more with the Illini of the North and confine our attention to Egypt. After all, only about ninety per cent of the state's population is in the northern half of Illinois.

Many paragraphs have been written about Egypt by great men ere I came along. Dickens, for example. He looked at Egypt from two directions when he was traveling in America. First he passed the southern boundary by boat, and the gladsome shore of Egypt caused him to write:

The trees were stunted in their growth; the banks were low and flat; the settlements and log cabins fewer in number: their inhabitants more wan and wretched than any we had encountered yet. No songs of birds were in the air, no pleasant scents, no moving lights and shadows from swift passing clouds. Hour after hour, the changeless glare of the hot, unwinking sky, shone upon the same monotonous objects. Hour after hour, the river rolled along, as wearily and slowly as the time itself.

At length . . . we arrived at a spot so much more desolate than any we had yet beheld, that the forlornest places we had

131

passed were, in comparison with it, full of interest. At the junction of the two rivers, on ground so flat and low and marshy, that at certain seasons of the year it is inundated to the house-tops, lies a breeding-place of fever, ague, and death . . . A dismal swamp, on which the half-built houses rot away . . . teeming, then, with rank unwholesome vegetation, in whose baleful shade the wretched wanderers who are tempted hither, droop, and die, and lay their bones . . . a place without one single quality, in earth or air or water, to commend it; such is this dismal Cairo.

It is difficult to believe, but I do think Charles Dickens misused the comma several times in the passages cited above. At least I would have left some of the commas out where he put them in, and put in a few where he left them out. Oh well, every man to his own style!

Mr. Dickens went on to St. Louis, where in time he announced that he would enjoy having a look at a prairie. Nothing was too good for him, so they took him across the river into Illinois where they had some prairies. He wrote extensively about that journey. For example:

We had a pair of very strong horses but travelled at the rate of little more than a couple of miles an hour, through one unbroken slough of black mud and water. It had no variety but in dept. Now it was only half over the wheels, now it hid the axletree, and now the coach sank down in it almost to the windows. The air resounded in all directions with the loud chirping of the frogs, who, with the pigs, (a coarse, ugly breed, as unwholesome-looking as though they were the spontaneous growth of the country), had the whole scene to themselves. Here and there, we passed a log hut; but the wretched cabins were wide apart and thinly scattered, for though the soil is very rich in this place few people can exist in such deadly atmosphere. On either side of the track, if it deserves the name, was the thick bush; and everywhere was stagnant, slimy, rotten, filthy water.

What did he expect, brandy? I have an idea that Dickens was looking at a portion of Egypt when he had those thoughts, and if my surmise is correct, I'm a little sore about it. After all, this is my own, my native land. If that bum didn't like it over here, why didn't he pack his duds and get to hell back where he came from! I certainly wish I had been around at the time, so I could have gone and had a look at Poop Hill, or whatever the name of the place was where *he* lived. We've simply got to put a stop to these god-dern Englishmen coming around with their noses in the air, and spats on, and unable to even talk the English language, and yet undertaking to tell us what is wrong with our way of life. Somerset Maugham, I warn you! Stay away from Egypt!

So much for Mr. Dickens. Let us turn to the writings of William Cowper Brann, who was known as Brann the Iconoclast. He was born in Coles County, Illinois, and spent his boyhood in those parts. Years later, recalling the way things were in his native state, he wrote:

To call a man a "son of Egypt" was considered an unforgivable affront to his family, and meant a fight or a footrace. It is a popular idea that, south of Centralia, the employment of the people consists in catching bull-heads and crawfish, frying out rattlesnake oil as an antidote for rheumatism, shaking with "buck-ager," drinking "sasafrack" tea, chawin natural leaf and expectorating the juice at a knothole. The "Egyptians" are generally thought to be immoral, but lacking sufficient vigor to break the Seventh Commandment; hungry, but too lazy to work and too cowardly to steal; lousy, yet lacking sufficient intelligence to scratch for relief. And, truth to tell, this portrait of Southern Illinois was no caricature a third of a century ago.

For some strange reason I'm beginning to get a little depressed about my origin; and I'm thinking that a little research is a dangerous thing. The observations I have cited don't seem to be a bit complimentary to the sod from which I sprang. Let us look further. Here is somebody named Dr. John Merritte Driver, who wrote a book called *Purple Peaks Remote*. This gentleman, probably a syringe-holder for an unlicensed veterinarian, chose to evaluate my people as follows:

The society in Southern Illinois is loud, conceited, sometimes coarse and vulgar. It is given to display and vanity. It is what we sometimes call "raw." The best literature is not in vogue, except in isolated instances, and the music that calls forth the most vociferous applause is of the "coon" and ragtime order. The young lady who can make the most noise on the piano and execute the most difficult composition with the greatest rapidity, regardless of expression, or the thought or purpose of the composer, is hailed as the greatest pianist.

On the streets, they bawl at each other, in the home they shout across the room, and when they laugh one is reminded of Balaam's faithful beast. The dare, the bet, the bank book are yet the great and all determinative denominators.

Says who? Says a horse doctor's assistant with the nerve to write a book called *Purple Peaks Remote*.

I have a volume called *The Handy-Book of Literary Curiosities*, and in it I find this:

EGYPT—a sobriquet applied to the southern portion of the State of Illinois—a figurative allusion to the Egyptian darkness of ignorance and immorality that was anciently credited to this section. But a more honorable explanation is that the extreme fertility of the soil made it the only portion of Illinois to escape the corn-famine of 1835, whence inhabitants of neighboring regions went down, as of old they went down into Egypt, to buy and carry back corn.

But enough of what these lardheads thought about southern Illinois. Obviously the time was ripe for me to come along and give the world a true picture of Egypt as it is and as it was.

Egypt has produced some great men and attracted others. Remember old Pontiac? After stirring up all that trouble, old Pontiac decided to get drunk for a while, and, looking around for a likely place for his bender, chose Egypt and took up residence at a place called Cahokia, which sounds like someone clearing his throat.

Pontiac had a granddaughter named Elizabeth living with him at Cahokia, and this Elizabeth, when she wasn't busy feeding alka-seltzers to her grandfather, found time to get involved with an Englishman named Williamson. There must have been some monkey business in their relationship because Pontiac was soon threatening to scalp Williamson clear down to his sternum. The Englishman grew frightened and went out and hired a Peoria Indian to eliminate Pontiac. So one night Pontiac went out in the woods to practice walking pigeon-toed or some such thing, being plastered at the time, and the Peoria Indian crept up behind him and knocked him in the head. Thus, in Egypt, the glorious career of a great chieftain came to an end. The entire story is of especial interest to me because my agent has an automobile called a Pontiac in which I am frequently a passenger.

I have already mentioned that William Jennings Bryan was a product of Egypt. So was William E. Borah, who grew up on a farm near Fairfield. He was against tobacco and liquor and never learned to drive an automobile.

Burl Ives is from Illinois, and while I don't believe that he came from Egypt, he talks as if he did. He is something of a character and once was a member of the Hoboes of America, Inc. Finally the movies discovered Mr. Ives to be a great singer of ballads and gave him a handsome contract. The Hoboes of America, Inc., in emergency session, promptly expelled him on the grounds that he had been "charged with and found guilty of steady work."

What an assemblage of prominent persons has come out of Egypt! Frank Willard, creator of Moon Mullins, was born in Anna. Elzie Crisler Segar, creator of Popeye, came out of

Chester. Then consider the little town of Cobden. Agnes Ayres, who once played opposite Rudolph Valentino, was born in Cobden, and a man named Parker Earl of that town is said to have invented a thing which inspired someone else to invent the refrigerator car. Prince Mike Romanoff, an individual who is not Prince Mike Romanoff, lived for a few years in Egypt when he was young.

Egypt can even lay claim to Robert G. Ingersoll. Egypt, in fact, does. This is a thing that passeth my understanding, inasmuch as organized religion is a powerful element throughout the length and narrowness of Egypt, as it is elsewhere in our land; yet the Egyptians boast of the fact that the great agnostic lived five years in their midst. He was around eighteen when he arrived in the company of his father, who was an itinerant preacher. He lived for a while in Mount Vernon, not far from my birthplace, and he sang the glories of his new home by describing it as "a very miserable part of the world." He spoke feelingly of the texture of the Egyptian countryside, made up chiefly of mud. He went to Metropolis, a town on the Ohio River, to teach school. One evening he was sitting around with some of the townspeople when the discussion turned on baptism. This has always been a topic for lively disputation in Egypt. It is not, however, a question of whether one is for or against baptism; the arguments develop over methods and technique. Men have had their teeth loosened for contending in favor of triple immersion as against a single ducking; people have quit speaking to each other because one argued that baptismal water has curative powers while the other said such a theory was nothing but old nuts; bitter feuds that have lasted for generations have been started by controversy over whether it is proper for a person being baptized to hold his nose. Even the quantity of water employed in a standard-gauge baptism has at times brought conflict. In my prowlings through the confused history of McLeansboro, I found that my native town once harbored a group of worshipers called the Forty Gallon Baptists.

Robert Ingersoll sat that night in Metropolis listening to the wise old people of the community argue about baptism.

He remained discreetly silent until someone finally turned to him and asked him what he thought of baptism.

"Baptism?" he repeated, as though he hadn't been listening. "I think baptism is a good thing—with soap."

As of that moment he was no longer the local teacher, no longer a local resident. The suddenness of his dismissal caught him so short that he had to walk all the way to his folks' home in Marion, fifty miles to the north. Later on he became a lawyer. Since success in the law often depends on a talent for glib talk, and since Ingersoll was a talker to who-laid-the-chunk, he became a successful lawyer; and as soon as he became successful he got out of Egypt. He figured, I suppose, that in leaving Egypt he was improving his condition. But guess where he went. Peoria.

Let it not be said that the people of Egypt are dull-witted and lacking in ingenuity. They invented Memorial Day; at least they claim they invented it. There are people in Georgia who will give them an argument; the *Egyptian Key* iterates and reiterates that the first Memorial Day was celebrated at Carbondale in 1866. After the graves in Woodlawn Cemetery had been decorated, everyone adjourned to a grove west of town and had fun—hogs furnished by the Dillinger boys, bread by John Borger.

I could go on piling up the evidence of Egypt's superiority for hours. Egypt has the only east-and-west mountain range in the United States. Other regions have to get along with mountain ranges that run north and south. Egypt's uncommon mountains, a range of hills crossing the southern part of Illinois, are genuine Ozarks. I have to admit that I didn't know about them until I made this trip—never once heard that Egypt had some Ozarks. I always thought they belonged exclusively to Missouri and Arkansas, and it pleased me immensely to learn that I am an Ozarkian. I may even start a radio program in opposition to Lum and Abner, designed for people who have that dull, headachy, ache-all-over feeling, including myself.

As for Egypt and literature, here I am compelled to cringe slightly. Egypt doesn't have a spectacular record of letters, although the state of Illinois is without a peer in this direction. Nonetheless, the whole tradition of Illinois literature stems from Egypt because the first person ever to write a novel in the state did so at Shawneetown. Her name was Sarah Marshall Hayden and her first novel was titled *Florence De Lisle*. It was about "the evils of early engagements." The more I consider that descriptive phrase, the less I make of it.

As for the remainder of the state, let me say that I am proud to be a Sucker, or Prairie. Let the Hoosiers beller their heads off about Indiana's great literary traditions, and I'll match them hack for hack. Let them yip about Riley and Tarkington, Nicholson and Ade, and I'll hit them between the eyes with some *substantial* people—Carl Sandburg and Ernest Hemingway, John Dos Passos and Finley Peter Dunne. I'll show them that their Mr. Dreiser learned to write in Illinois. Let them talk of their Lloyd C. Douglas and I'll dazzle them with Elbert Hubbard. If they so much as mention Elizabeth Hack of Boggstown, Indiana (*Saul of Tarsus*), I'll come right back at them with Lida Brown McMurry of Polo, Illinois (*Classic Stories for the Little Ones*). Let Indiana try to match Carl and Mark Van Doren who came from Vermilion County; or Frank Norris, Don Marquis, Mary Austin, Floyd Dell, and Rachel Crothers. Maybe they haven't heard of Harold Sinclair, but I can tell them that he wrote a book called *American Years* that's a far better historical novel than anything Lew Wallace ever put together. And just to make certain that those cocky Hoosiers cease their boastful shouting and get back to their whittling in the Odd Fellows Hall, I give them Vincent Sheean, Allan Nevins, Archibald MacLeish, Albert Halper, John Gunther, Kenneth Fearing, James T. Farrell, James Gould Cozzens, Franklin P. Adams, Vincent Starrett, Margaret Ayer Barnes . . . and even Irna Phillips of Chicago, who can keep five different soap operas going on the radio without missing a meal.

When I get this unwieldy caravan to McLeansboro I'll be able to point out additional people of distinction who not only were and are Egyptians but who lived right in the very town where I was born. We're almost ready, in fact, to proceed to Hamilton County, but first one item must be cleared from the agenda. I feel that I must explain why I never did get to Decatur.

Decatur is a city up near the middle of the state, and I spent several of my formative years in it. My memories of Decatur form a sort of goofy montage. I know that as a child I attended Pugh School and that kids from other schools were accustomed to taunting us with cries of "Pew! Pew!" uttered while holding their nasty little noses. I know I lived on King Street but I don't think I'd ever be able to identify the house if I went in search of it. I know that while I was in Decatur I believe that if you saw an owl in a tree and you started walking around and around that tree, the owl would follow you with his eyes, continually turning his head until he wrung his own neck. I know I believed that because I tried it.

For a period I was a boy scout in Decatur but never progressed beyond the tenderfoot class. And while I was a boy scout a major fraud was perpetrated against me. In Fairview Park there stands a log cabin which is called the "Lincoln Log Cabin Courthouse." It was the custom in the time of my childhood, and may still be, for scoutmasters to take groups of their knot tiers out to this cabin and spend the night there. I went on one such expedition. The cabin, as I remember, was a one-room affair, and after we had all disposed ourselves around the rough floor our scoutmaster gave us a solemn lecture. He said that the walls and the floor and the ceiling were hallowed by the spirit of Abraham Lincoln; that Abe used to pace these floors as he argued a legal case. It was a great and wonderful and beautiful thing that we should be permitted to sleep in such a sanctified place, and he said that we should always remember it and tell our grandchildren about it.

I did remember it, down through the years, and sometimes dwelt upon it in my mind and felt reverent toward Abraham Lincoln because I had been close to him in spirit that night. But that scoutmaster was lying. Long afterward I happened to come across the real story of that cabin. True enough, it was the town's original courthouse and at one time stood in Decatur's business district. And there was a reason for calling it the "Lincoln Log Cabin Courthouse." It was erected in 1829 and it was associated with the name Lincoln by virtue of an entry found in the early records of Macon County—a notation showing that one John Hanks received $9.87 for "chinking and daubing" the courthouse. Now get the connection with Abe. John Hanks, who chinked and daubed, was the cousin of Abraham Lincoln's mother. For all I know, Abe himself never got within miles of the cabin where I couldn't even sleep for all the patriotic sentiment swelling within me. When I found out the truth I was so mad that if I could have got my hands on the scoutmaster, I'd have chinked and daubed *him*.

Also in Fairview Park, I was once a participant in a wand drill.

But I didn't go to Decatur. I could invent a variety of reasons for not finishing the job I had started, but if you want the truth—by the time I got through with Egypt I was fed up with the scenes of my childhood.

So let us now proceed to McLeansboro. My heart beats faster as the Plymouth speeds us southward. And as we draw closer to the town I burst into song—"Git out th' way fer Ole Dan Tucker"—a nursery rhyme my father used to sing to me when I was a child, just before slapping me to sleep.

Chapter 11

In *Look Homeward, Angel* Thomas Wolfe was writing the story of his own early life, and in the beginning of the book he did some A-No.-1 remembering. He remembered many things that happened to him, or around him, when he was three years old, and even younger; he even recorded the thoughts and sensations that came to him as he lay in his crib. I suppose that is a form of literary license, but I don't believe there is much integrity attached to it. Thomas Wolfe was a most unusual guy and influenced the writing of every contemporary author in America except me. Maybe he did remember his didy days, but I'm inclined to think he made it all up. This literary license gag can sometimes be overdone. I've never been able to understand, for example, how one man writing a biography about another man who is dead can set down the thoughts of his subject during childhood and adolescence. I couldn't do it about myself, because I can't remember what I thought about, if anything.

Driving from Mount Vernon toward McLeansboro that spring day, I performed some remarkable feats of concentration, trying to remember as much as I could about my birthplace. In Mount Vernon I made one final effort to get a look at an *Illinois Guide*. I really needed it. I needed to be briefed on McLeansboro and Hamilton County. I needed just a little bit of preparation for the emotional adventure that lay before me.

The Mount Vernon library was closed and I had to go on without getting a look at the guide. I might as well report, right here, that I didn't find a copy of the book until I got back to New York. The White Plains Library let me have its copy for a while. It contains more than seven hundred pages and costs five bucks and is an admirable work copyrighted in the name of the governor of Illinois. I would like to pound him over the head with it. In all its pages there is not a single mention of McLeansboro. The words "Hamilton County" cannot be found in it. The big folding map in the back of the book is a clever work of cartography; McLeansboro is not on it. My home town is a county seat and has a population of three thousand, but the goons who got up the guide by-passed it. McLeansboro produced a governor of the state, a couple of famous jockeys, a man who grew up to become manager of the St. Louis Cardinals; and every woman, man, and child in the city of Springfield could be boiled alive in the oil that has been produced in Hamilton County. Yet the legmen of the *Illinois Guide* skirted the borders of the county as if mad dogs and rattlesnakes were loose on its highways. The town of Hooppole (226 pop.) is described in detail, and the town of New Burnside (299 pop.), and many other towns with scarcely enough population to make up a good game of Kelly pool; but no McLeansboro. I don't know how many hours I spent or how many booksellers and librarians I pestered throughout the trip trying to get that guide just so I could have some basic information about McLeansboro. What was all that fancy rhetoric I tossed around earlier in this book about those guides? Phooey on the WPA—the dumb shovel-leaners!

So it was that as I approached McLeansboro I had to depend on fragments of memory; I had to make an effort to piece those fragments together and make some sort of a picture. As to the physical properties of the town, I could only recall the square and the courthouse.

A few things came back to me, dreamlike. I was in the front yard of our home when they carried a neighbor lady out of her house and loaded her into a black wagon. I was

told that this lady was being taken away because she had gone crazy. I didn't even know what crazy meant at that time. I have since learned.

I was taken to my first movie, which was shown in a tent. There was a scene in which the villain threw the heroine bodily from a speeding train. The heroine was represented by an exceedingly crude dummy, and as the villain lifted this dummy into the air and prepared to hurl it off the train, I arose from my folding chair and screamed: "He's got our hard girl!" We had a hired girl at that time, but we didn't have her the next day because my outburst was all over town by bedtime and the hired girl seemed to take offense at being identified with the dummy.

I have a faint recollection of falling into an empty cistern and remaining there for a long time before I was found. And I remembered being taken to the Home Place and what great and wonderful expeditions those were—traveling out to visit my grandparents and sometimes spending a whole day in those remote parts. Soon I would learn that this far-off Home Place stands on the edge of McLeansboro and was the equivalent of about three city blocks from the house where I lived.

Names of disembodied personalities came back, probably through my having heard my folks speak of them, names such as Turrentine, Stelle, Shephard, Epperson, Campbell, Wright, McNabb, Davis, Blades, Echols, Utley, Biggerstaff, Dailey, Eckley, Daniels, Ledbetter, Cloud, Lasater, and Tevis. The names were familiar to me, but there was not a one of them that I could associate with the person to whom it belonged.

We came into McLeansboro from the west, past highway billboards most of which were advertising God, and arrived at the square. Traffic around the square is one-way, counterclockwise, and my first act was to violate this regulation. I drove against the grain no more than fifty feet when a policeman yelled at me and came bounding into the street and gave me colorful hell. I apologized and pleaded ignorance and he let me go. I got turned around, drove halfway around the square, and headed into an angle-parking place. An old guy in dirty overalls was sitting on the curb at the spot where I was trying to park, his legs sprawled out onto the pavement, a newspaper in his hands. I eased the car in, inch by inch, figuring he would look up and see me coming and remove himself from the curb. I got up to within about two feet of his shoes and then gently tapped the horn. He bounced a yard or two off the curb, glared at me, started mumbling some bad language, and resumed his seat. Danged if *he* was gonna move! For a moment I thought I would make an issue of it, but then I remembered that I was a complete stranger to this town and its people—that this curb sitter might be the mayor or the sheriff or the county judge; so I backed out and went on around and parked in front of a movie house where a double bill was playing, both Westerns.

After that I made the complete circuit of the square on foot, admiring the new courthouse standing where the old brick one had been. Most of the McLeansboro stores, facing the square, have shed roofs extending out over the sidewalk. These are constructed of wood or galvanized iron and supported by iron poles, and they reflect the Southern traditions of the town. Subsequently I told a McLeansboro merchant that I considered these shed roofs to be unsightly, and he agreed with me, and I asked why they were not torn down.

"When it rains here," he said, "it rains cats and dogs. And when it comes on summer, you never see the like of such blazing heat. If we was to tear down them roofs, we'd have a revolution on our hands. Where could people loaf at if they didn't have that protection from the sun and rain?"

I have an assortment of aunts and cousins in McLeansboro, and one cousin, Veronica Hassett, had been notified of our impending visit and she was to get us a hotel room. We drove to her house and found out that there was no hotel room available. The town has but one hotel and it contains perhaps a dozen rooms, and these rooms had been engaged for weeks ahead. We had reached McLeansboro, I learned, during a momentous week. The coming Saturday was to be "John Stelle Day"—the biggest, most splendid week in all McLeansboro's history. The town was going to honor its most famous son—John Stelle, who at that time was National Commander of the American Legion. Stelle was born and grew up in McLeansboro and still counts it as his home, being a gentleman farmer with a place just outside the town. He had been governor of Illinois and he had lately been much in the news through his quarrels with General Bradley of the Veterans Administration.

On the very day we reached McLeansboro they started

putting up the bunting for John Stelle Day, and an extraordinary amount of pride was taken in this operation. Everyone bragged about the fact that this bunting was the very same bunting, provided by a St. Louis firm, which was used to decorate the streets of Fulton, Missouri, some months earlier when both President Truman and Winston Churchill visited that town.

The celebration of John Stelle Day was to be centered at the fairgrounds. The governors of Illinois and Indiana were to be present. Trainloads of legionnaires were to come to McLeansboro. There was to be a pony race, a plug race, a mule race, an old fiddlers' contest, a square dance, fireworks, and—glory of glories!—the National Barn Dance radio program was to be broadcast right smack dab from the McLeansboro Fairgrounds, featuring such celebrated personalities as Arkie the Arkansas Woodchopper, Lulu Belle and Scotty, the Hoosier Hot Shots, and even Joe Kelly himself.

In spite of the lack of hotel accommodations, we stuck to our resolution not to bed down in the homes of relatives and found a room at the residence of Orlin J. Davis, a retired merchant. Mr. Davis was an old-timer in McLeansboro and his house was built in the year that I was born and, at that time, was considered to be a show place. He was a widower and lived alone in the big house and had plenty of room. Before we moved in one of my aunts gave me a little talk on what a nice man he was. "Orlin," she said, "used to give readings. He was a James Whitcomb Riley reader and one of the best." I think, also, that he's the one she said used to be quite a flat-foot waltzer.

Once we were settled in the Davis house I set to work finding out all I could about the town of my origin. I delayed visiting the actual house where I was born and the other houses where my family had lived and the Home Place; I wanted to get better acquainted with my town before launching upon those sentimental adventures.

I called at the office of the local weekly newspaper, the *Times-Leader,* and met a young man named Casey Dempsey, lately back from the wars. He showed me where the files of old McLeansboro newspapers were stacked and told me to help myself. From those old papers and from talks with

146

McLeansboro people and from subsequent conversations with my father I found out that I was born in the most interesting town in the United States—a town that is tremendously interesting because its story is so dull. Dull, I mean, to people like the myopic bums who put together the *Illinois Guide,* but never dull for a moment to me.

I was told that McLeansboro was a town without a history —that nothing had ever happened in McLeansboro that was worth recording. Such flapdoodle! What about th' hangin'? What about the burning of the courthouse? What about Acey Todd and his hallucinations? What about Coxey's Army?

The first settlers of Hamilton County came up from the South about 1815, built themselves dirt-floor cabins, and settled down to a life of eating hominy. By 1818 there were enough of them to get up prayer meetings, and it is recorded that at one of these meetings an old Negro walked in, a complete stranger, and preached a sermon. His appearance made such an impression that the settlers put him to work teaching a little school. Thus the first sermon ever preached in the county was preached by a Negro, and he taught the first school. There are no Negroes today in McLeansboro; I don't think I ever saw one until after we moved to Decatur.

The history of those early days is extremely fragmentary. I found a brief account of a nut by the name of Indian Charley, who showed up and started complaining against some people named Gray—said they had stolen his bell. Indian Charley spent several years going from cabin to cabin and bellyaching about his bell, and asking people if they would kindly go with him and help him kill all the Grays. When at last it became apparent that nobody was going to join him in the massacre, he gave up the project and disappeared. It is not stated what kind of a bell Indian Charley had, or what he did with it when he had it, or why the Grays would want to steal it. This entire incident, I must confess, is on the negative side; but I bring it in as evidence that partly supports the theory that McLeansboro is weak in the history department. If Indian Charley had turned up in Kansas or Colorado or Indiana or Tennessee, and there had been some Grays in those places, there would have likely been a massacre, with tomahawkings and cabins going up in flames and infants snatched from their mothers' breasts and General Custer arriving at the crucial moment. Frankly, I'm a little disappointed in Indian Charley—he could have made these pages so much more lively and dramatic. What the hell did he want with the bell in the first place?

The first people of Hamilton County had no town, but they wanted one. So along came a certain Dr. William McLean and some of his friends. They acquired a large tract of land, and in 1821 Dr. McLean himself decided he would contribute twenty acres for a townsite. In that same year the settlement was platted and Dr. McLean built the first house on it.

For a while they didn't know what name to give their town. There was talk of calling it Rector, after a surveyor named John Rector who did the original survey of the county. There is a Rector Creek named for this man, but I bring him into the story solely because of his obituary notice. In an old *History of Illinois* I found a mention of the fact that he had been killed by Indians while at work on his survey. His obituary, as printed in that history, is singularly appropriate for a surveyor. It says:

John Rector died May 25, 1805, at the section corner of Sections 21, 22, 23 and 28; buried from this corner, south 62 degrees west 72 poles, small stone monument, stone quarry northwest 150 yards.

But they didn't name the town Rector; they toyed with some names out of Greek mythology, considering Penelope and Hector and Agamemnon and Argus and Bellerophon and all that sort of foolishness. Then occurred an incident that strikes me as being mildly wonderful. The founding fathers were engaged in a discusion of possible names when along came an old character who, as the historian puts it, had "partaken too freely of tanglefoot." I don't think that the historian meant that the old guy had been eating flypaper. He listened a bit to the discussion and then spoke his piece. He said: "Boys, 'y god, call 'er after Ole Doc McLean here." And so they did.

In later years John B. Kinnear attempted a historical

sketch of the town, telling how it had grown from "the darkest and vilest pit, where the slime of the serpents would pour, to a thriving temperance town of two thousand." McLeansboro—given its name by a drunk—has been a dry town throughout most of its history.

In Mr. Dempsey's newspaper I found the intelligence that Pinkney McNabb was the first mayor of McLeansboro, the first typewriter in town was owned by Ottis McNabb, and "Lena Powell owned the first piano, a Steinway brought to Cincinnati by boat and to McLeansboro by ox team."

When I told my father about these matters he exploded. That note about the first piano was the thing that set him to cussing. He insisted that Lena Powell was *not* the owner of the first piano. The first piano belonged to the Allen family—my own people. Pop said there was no question about it. Once when he was roaming around in Arkansas he got into conversation with a hobo who, it turned out, came originally from southern Illinois. This hobo told Pop that he was not a bum by nature, that he came from good people, and that his people had contributed to the culture of southern Illinois.

"My ancestors," he said, "hauled the very first piano into southern Illinois and delivered it to the Allen family in McLeansboro."

"Why, Jesus Christ," my father said to him, "I married into that family."

Pop told me that the few people who have written historical bits about McLeansboro have neglected the Allens to a shameful degree—that Joe Allen, the first of the tribe to land in McLeansboro, was a real-estate speculator who owned about half the county, and donated the land on which the first public school was built, and operated two or three different stores and so on.

Maybe this Joe Allen, who was my great-grandfather, fell on evil days in the end, because his name figures in a saying that is still current in the town. One of my relatives explained to me that "Old Joe Allen liked to . . . well, he liked to rest. He would sit all day on his porch, every day. Once a friend of his came along and asked him what he was doing these days. He said, 'I'm helpin' Joe Allen.' That remark went all over town, and ever since then whenever a man is out of work and loafing or just plain lazy, he says he's helpin' Joe Allen."

Pop said it may have been true that Joe Allen was inclined to laziness, but, by God, Joe Allen had the first piano in McLeansboro and the hell with Lena Powell.

Historians, for some reason, attach great importance to first pianos. In my reading of Midwestern history I am constantly running into accounts of first pianos. Chicago historians say that a man named Beaubien had the first piano in that town, if not in Illinois. He had his first piano in 1834, and I don't think his claim will stand up against either Lena Powell's or Joe Allen's. In Vevay, Indiana, they have a first piano on exhibition in the local library, a Clemati, said to have been brought from England in 1817. It belonged to a girl named Mary Wright, daughter of an aristocratic but impoverished English family. Her folks brought her, with her piano, to the wilds of Indiana, where they settled in a rough cabin. Mary had been deserted by her English boy friend and she was daffy with grief about it. She secluded herself in the attic of the cabin except for one day a week. On that day she'd wash under her arms and attire herself in court dress and jewels, then come down the ladder from the attic, play a concert on the piano, and then go back up the ladder to sulk for another week. She did this for forty years without ever learning a single new composition and without ever having the piano tuned and then she died, and I imagine there was not a great deal of mourning among the neighbors.

It looks, therefore, as if Indiana had a first piano before Illinois; I don't intend to yield, however, from the contention that Joe Allen had McLeansboro's first.

Joe Allen's son, C. J. Allen, popularly known as "Cad" Allen, was my grandfather. Cad was a sort of jack-of-all-trades around McLeansboro. He was a member of the volunteer fire department although he didn't occupy the eminence of my other grandfather, Caleb Smith, who was First Plugman of Hose Company No. 1. I have heard it said, though, that nobody enjoyed going to a good fire so much as Cad Allen. A story is told in the family of how in the middle of a summer night the fire alarm sounded. Cad leaped out of bed and began throwing on his clothes. He was all ready to rush out of the house when one of his young daughters began wailing in another room, saying she wanted a drink of water. Cad went to the kitchen and got a glass of water and took it to her and had to stand by until she had finished it. Again he started for the door, but my grandmother called him back and asked him to turn down the wick in the lamp near her bed. He came back and turned it down and for the third time started for the door, but halfway there he stopped and announced loudly: "Now if they's anything *else* anybody wants, just speak up, because I ain't in no hurry a-tall!"

Fire and fire fighting bulks large in the history of McLeansboro as it does, I suppose, in every small town, and the burning of the courthouse is a landmark in that history. My father has often told me how in the days of his youth there was always a group of young men in the town famous for their meanness. They drank liquor and fought with their fists and in the eyes of the respectable citizens were a disgrace to the community. They were known as the town toughs. I asked Pop if he was one of them, and he denied it vigorously. "Hell no," he said, "I was a respectable citizen. But I could lick anybody my size and I could outdrink all of them."

One springtime a man arrived in McLeansboro with the latest type of fire-fighting engine. It was a pumper which had to be operated by crews of men who worked on either side of the machine. A hose would be dropped into a well, the firemen would start pumping, and a fairly strong stream of water could be produced. It was the hope of the man who brought in the engine, of course, that he would be able to sell it to the town. Everyone was greatly excited about it, including the town toughs.

"Seems like," said one of them, "that this'd be a good time to burn down the courthouse."

The courthouse apparently was an odious edifice to these young men, a symbol of the law. If anything had to be burned in order that the fire-engine salesman might demonstrate his pumper, then it should be the courthouse. So that very night they set fire to the courthouse, and it was burning briskly by the time the new engine arrived. There was a well on the courthouse lawn and the salesman dropped his hose into it. Volunteer firemen lined up on either side of the pumper and went to work. At this stage in the proceedings the town toughs decided that no joke is so excellent that it can't be improved upon. Several of them crept up to the well and cut holes in the hose. The firemen pumped furiously, but not even a trickle came from the nozzle, and the courthouse burned to the ground.

Chapter 12

My father's present profession is that of handy man in a tourist camp. He works in a roadside cabin resort on Highway One near the town of Laurel, Maryland. He has a deep and abiding respect for sinful people though he is remarkably free of sin himself. Laurel is a town with a race track attached to it, and in season and out many horse players are to be found in its borders; yet Pop, so far as I know, has never ventured a dime on a race. His weekly salary at the tourist camp is far from munificent, but he loves his job and refuses to leave it for anything better, such as total retirement. He points out to me that he has his own sleeping quarters free, and all his meals, and what is most important —all the beer he can drink. This in return for tinkering with the plumbing, fixing the iceboxes when they go haywire, helping out in the kitchen when the cook gets drunk, and renting cabins to tourists when the boss wants to go away.

Elsewhere I have written some things about Pop and I have always made an effort to quote him correctly, for he speaks the language that is used throughout Egypt and, in slight variation, throughout the Midwest. Some of my relatives have been displeased over "the way you make Pop talk," contending that in quoting him I make him sound ignorant, which he isn't.

Nonetheless, I intend to go on quoting him exactly as he talks, so far as I'm able to do it. Everyone, I suppose, is aware of the current agitation among groups of liberal writers to do away with all dialect writing. Today, if you quote an Italian-American precisely, or a Negro, or a Jew, or a Dodger fan, setting down in print the exact construction these people give their phrases and sentences, you identify yourself with the forces of Fascist reaction; you are looked upon as a narrow person, heavy-laden with intolerance. In other words, when a writer interviews Joe Louis, he should go back to his typewriter and set down the thoughts and opinions of Joe Louis in the language that Gene Tunney uses, and the same for Primo Carnera, and Sam Goldwyn, and Red Barber, and Gregory Ratoff, and my pop. Carried to its logical conclusion, this movement would eliminate from American literature such performers as Roark Bradford, Arthur Kober, and Ring Lardner. If restrictions are to be imposed on dialect writing, they must cover the whole field; you can't very well say that one dialect is permissible while another is not. It looks to me as if we were headed for our own little Burning of the Books, and that the bonfire will have to include the writings of Bradford, Kober, and Lardner, along with much of Mark Twain, and Finley Peter Dunne, and Octavus Roy Cohen, and Erskine Caldwell, and some of John Steinbeck (certainly that wonderful *Tortilla Flat*), and our old friend James Whitcomb Riley. The list could be stretched out a mile. It is my opinion that the people who are agitating against the use of dialect are shortsighted even though their motives are good. Just recently I witnessed a motion picture involving an all-Negro cast. The dialogue, from beginning to end, was as close to the dialogue of Amos 'n Andy as it is possible to get and equally close to the dialogue to be heard in the bar at the Hotel Theresa in Harlem. I could no more set down a story as told by a Negro maid in my home in the language of Gabriel Heatter than I could set down a story told by Pop employing the phrasing of Franklin D. Roosevelt. If the boys put over their campaign, it looks like tree surgery or running an addressograph or a milk route for me.

Just before I started writing this book I got into my car and drove down to see my father. I talked him into taking a leave of absence from his pipe wrenches and going on a trip with me. We drove south, wandering around in the Carolinas and Georgia, and on the street in Augusta, I asked an elderly Negro in overalls if he could direct us to our hotel.

"Indeed," he said, "I shall be pleased no end to be of assistance to you. See yon intersection? Turn your motorcar to the left, keeping in mind that you are progressing in a westerly direction, and proceed perhaps a quarter of a mile, when you will see a beautiful white edifice, testimonial to the progressiveness of our glorious civilization here in the South. I trust you will have no difficulty."

We loafed around that hotel for days, and I spent most of my time pumping my father, trying to get McLeansboro stuff out of him. He told a million stories, but not many of them had anything to do with McLeansboro, or Illinois, for that matter. For example, he told about an incident at a railroad underpass somewhere—I've forgotten whether he actually witnessed it or just read about it.

A huge van had been driven into the underpass. The roof of the van was just a trifle too high for clearance; it struck the girders supporting the bridge, and the driver found himself in a bad situation. He tried to back out of the trap, but the van was wedged tightly in its position and wouldn't budge. Soon other truck drivers and motorists were congregated at the spot and there were weighty deliberations over a possible method of getting that truck loose.

The driver of the van was furious over his error in judgment, but he was the kind of a guy who takes his anger out on other people. He blamed the railroad for his plight and announced that if he had some dynamite he'd blow the goddam bridge to bits. At last it was decided that an acetylene torch was needed; he would cut away part of the girder to get his truck free.

At this point a boy, ten or twelve years old, spoke up.

"Listen, mister," he called out, "I know how you can get 'er out without much trouble."

"Beat it!" snarled the truck driver. "Get t' hell outa here!"

"It's simple," insisted the kid. "Let part of the air outa your tires and she'll clear that girder."

The van driver stared angrily at the kid for a moment,

then went for him and tried to slap him for his audacity in trying to solve a problem that had baffled grown men. The kid ducked and scampered away and, from a safe distance, watched with great satisfaction when, a bit later, the belligerent driver let air out of his tires and drove the van on through the underpass.

Whenever he did get to talking about McLeansboro, Pop's stories for the most part had little point to them, since he is not a writer like his son. He did tell me about a man named Acey Todd, who had a fixation. I am now going to quote Pop as accurately as I can; I do it with the knowledge that you, the reader of this book, no matter where you live in the United States, may someday be talking in the same fashion. My authority for this statement is Professor John Webster Spargo of Northwestern University, who recently completed a study of the evolution of language in this country. He found that the Southern drawl and the New England twang and all other dialects, save one, are disappearing from our national speech; and the speech of the Midwest is growing and spreading over the land, and someday people in Fort Worth, Texas, and Mobile, Alabama, and Bennington, Vermont, and in the Cub Room of the Stork Club, and even on Rex Stout's farm at Brewster, New York, will be talking the way Pop talks.

"Acey Todd," said my father, "was a little crazy. He was born in McLeansburr and lived there all his life, but he believed he come from Shawneetown. He'd have spells where he'd go around town tellin' everbody he come from Shawneetown and he was the toughest son-of-a-bitch on earth, and he might near *was*. This went on for years, and then finely Acey *did* go to Shawneetown. I guess he decided he had talked so much about it that he better try to make it true. Anyways, he went to Shawneetown and somewhere down there he got a hold of a horse. He rode that horse back to McLeansburr and come into town in the early evenin'. He had a pistol and he started racin' that horse up and down the streets and all around the square and across the courthouse lawn. Ever' time he saw a street light he'd shoot 'er out, and then he'd yell about how by God he come from Shawneetown and about how tough he was. It took might near all night to get Acey roped up and put in jail."

Pop also remembered the time when a portion of Coxey's Army came through McLeansboro. The town was warned a couple of weeks ahead of time that the Army was planning to camp overnight in a field on the outskirts of McLeansboro. The townspeople didn't quite understand what Coxey's Army was all about. "Army" meant only one thing to them—fightin'. The women of the town were especially alarmed, and under their worrisome goading the men got out their shotguns and rifles and spent a week at intensive target practice. All this shooting had a sort of hypnotic effect on the menfolks, and before long *they* were believing that an armed force was marching against their town and it was up to them to repel the invaders. Business houses closed down and some people started throwing up barricades and laying in supplies against the possibility of a long siege.

At last the Coxey followers arrived, piling off freight trains outside the town, armed with nothing more lethal than corncob pipes and buttonhooks. For a few hours the town lay quiet, its citizens awaiting the first awful assault, hidden in basements and attics. At last a scout from Coxey's Army got together with a sentry from the defending force and convinced the sentry that nobody was going to invade anything. The army was going to camp overnight and then move on toward Washington. Some of the more venturesome of the townspeople, including Pop, went out to see the camp; the others stuck to their houses, with shades drawn, until the danger was past. The next day the Coxey men went out south of town and rubbed soap on the rails of the L. & N. Along came a freight train; the locomotive wheels hit the soaped rails and started spinning. By the time the engine could get across the stretch of soaped rails, the Coxey warriors were all on board, and away they went.

The most famous incident in McLeansboro history, according to an evaluation made by my father, was "th' hangin'." A farmer at Piopolis named Fred Behme got into an argument with his wife about religion. I have no information on the exact nature of the argument, though it could possibly have been about the amount of water that should be used in a baptism. The Piopolis farmer disagreed with his wife so violently that he settled matters by knocking her on the head with a chunk of wood; then he took their youngest child out to the barn and lynched him between two mules. Never argue about religion.

Fred Behme was hanged amid great ceremony on the courthouse lawn in McLeansboro, and it has been said that every living person in Hamilton County, plus many from beyond its borders, attended the execution. That statement, of course, is an exaggeration. There were three boys—lads of an age when, you would think, no power on earth could keep them away from a hanging—who were missing from the immense crowd. One of these boys was Pop. A couple of days before the hanging he and two of his pals had a conference. They knew that every farmer, and every farmer's wife, and every hired hand in the whole county would be in McLeansboro to witness the edifying spectacle of a fellow man getting his neck cracked. What an opportunity to get some rabbits! All the farmers for miles around had forbidden rabbit shooting or any other kind of trespassing on their land, and the sport of killing rabbits was, in consequence, all but dying out in the county. Pop and his two friends waited until midmorning of Fred Behme's last day and then took their guns and started out. Everywhere they went they found deserted farms, and before they were finished they had killed 126 rabbits, which they carried back to town on long poles.

"In them days," Pop told me, "I had rather kill a rabbit any day than see a hangin'."

During my stay in McLeansboro, after I had done sufficient research to give me a fairly clear picture of the town as it had been in the past, I got to wondering why it was there at all. The McLeansboro Chamber of Commerce is not going to admire me for having such thoughts, but I had them, and if this book is to live through the ages, I must report them. The town was established before railroads had opened up the Midwest. Up to that time the only sensible settlements were those established on waterways. There was no beaten track anywhere near McLeansboro. Certainly there was no water, beyond a little crick that passes through the old Caleb Smith property and runs on through the town and is called the Rhine.

What on earth ever caused Dr. McLean and his friends to pick McLeansboro as the site for McLeansboro? Were they running from somebody? They couldn't possibly have known that the railroads would eventually penetrate to Egypt. That's what happened, of course, and that was the making of McLeansboro. The railroad was the chief factor in making a town out of almost nothing, yet the railroad

people had a difficult time getting themselves established in southern Illinois. They didn't lay down the standard-size rails that are in use today. Their first rails were flimsy strips of metal. They'd no more than get a stretch of these rails nailed down when somebody would come along and rip them up and take them away. The railroad people investigated this sabotage and discovered that the rails were being taken away by farmers, who had found that they made excellent sled runners.

A man who starts thinking that there is no reason why there ever should have been a town in which he was born is indulging in an unhealthy mental exercise. If he decides that there was no excuse for the town, logic leads him to the conclusion that there was no excuse for himself. This line of reasoning can lead to morbid maundering, and even suicide. This paragraph is getting into the realm of psychology, and while it may not be the best psychology in the world, I figure it's as good as Philip Wylie's, so I think I'll let it stand.

I thought about the apparent lack of logic behind the founding of McLeansboro until, a week or so later, I found myself in southern Missouri and had a look at a town called New Madrid, pronounced with the accent on Mad. Here is a town of approximately the same size as McLeansboro but with the significant attribute of having been founded on navigable water—the Mississippi River, no less.

As we have seen, McLeansboro, poorly located, with no reasonable excuse for the driving of the first stake, has had a rather dull existence, with the hangin' and the burning of the courthouse as highlights of its history. Not so New Madrid, with its ideal situation on the Mississippi. The story of New Madrid should be reassuring to the people of McLeansboro and make them happy that down through the years they have been able to take naps in the afternoon.

New Madrid started out as a French settlement, and the French called it Greasy Bend, because there was a bend in the river there. I don't know why they called it *Greasy* Bend, unless they buttered the banks of the Mississippi to keep it from changing its course. It did change its course, four or five times, ruining the town and necessitating a move to a better locality, or what was *thought* to be a better locality. In the early days the citizens lived in constant fear of river pirates, who practiced the arts of robbery and murder and who seemed to have an affinity for this particular town. Then, in 1811, on December sixteenth, came the earthquake. I have heard it said that the New Madrid earthquake was far and away the worst earthquake this country ever experienced and that San Francisco's vaunted disaster was no more than a stubbed toe in comparison to it. That New

Madrid earthquake was an earthquake with staying power. It let go with a crash and a bang on that first December day. And it shook and heaved and rumbled and belched every day thereafter for two years. *Every day for two years!* Why everyone didn't pick up and move to Montana, or Egypt, is a thing I cannot understand. During those two years a person couldn't walk down what was left of the street without standing a chance of having the earth heave open and spit noxious gas in his face and then gobble him up. It was a tough proposition to keep even a straight-back chair all in one piece. There were landslides, and the Mississippi behaved worse than usual, sending huge waves over its banks to engulf the shattered community. Many people, to be sure, did move away, but many more stayed on. They must have loved New Madrid.

At last the two years of earthquake were over, and the people who were left settled down to a life of comparative serenity, their peaceful existence no more to be disturbed by anything more serious than a ripsnorting flood or another changing of the river bed. They just did get settled down when the Fanatical Pilgrims arrived. This group comprised as fine a collection of nuts as I've ever heard about. They were religious people. When they first arrived at New Madrid they said they were looking for Jerusalem. If I had been there I'd have given them a road map and pointed east. They must have decided that New Madrid *was* Jerusalem, because they stayed. All of them wore tattered clothes. They believed it was sinful to wash their bodies; consequently they stunk. They didn't believe in labor, meaning work. They didn't believe in burying their dead (the book I have doesn't say what they did with them). They believed that they could fall out of a tree without hurting themselves. They ate nothing but mush and milk, which they put into a wooden bowl and sucked up through a hollow cornstalk.

Perhaps if they had gone off into their own neighborhood and behaved themselves, everything would have been all right. Personally, I would have tolerated them provided they settled far enough away from my house so I couldn't smell them. I'd even go out and visit them now and then with a clothespin on my nose, just for the pleasure of seeing them fall out of trees or watching them suck mush and milk through a cornstalk. But it appears that people of their nature just can't be satisfied to sit around, not working, admiring their old corpses. Without warning, these Fanatical Pilgrims would burst into a citizen's house and start yelling, "Repent! Repent!"

This practice may have led, in the end, to their expulsion from the community. If it did, I don't know about it, and the book doesn't say what ultimately happened to them. I have one thing in common with them—I do not believe in work, so I'm not going to travel all the way in to the New York Public Library to look it up.

Returning to McLeansboro, I asked several citizens to tell me what, in their estimation, was the most distinctive thing they knew about the town—what there was, in the story of McLeansboro, to brag about.

One of them, a man of Confederate leanings, told me that when the Civil War started and Illinois was ceded to the Northern cause, the people of Egypt let out a howl of protest. They were predominately rebel and they wanted to fight with the Confederates. There were big mass meetings in McLeansboro as well as in other Egyptian towns. Public feeling was being crystallized into a strong movement for secession. Egypt would secede from Illinois and become a separate state, called Egypt, and would fight with the South. Egypt's top politician at the time was John A. Logan, and he was in Congress; as soon as he heard about the disturbances at home he hurried back from Washington. He was a great orator and could sway sheep, so he rushed into Egypt and orated and talked everyone, or almost everyone, into sticking with Abe Lincoln. My McLeansboro informant said that if that damn Logan hadn't come back Egypt would have split off and become a separate state and maybe McLeansboro would have become the state capital. I'm not inclined to give this thing much serious consideration—there are too many "ifs" involved in it.

Another citizen answered my question by saying that the first air mail ever flown was launched from McLeansboro in 1912. Nice if true, but the claim lacks authenticity. The first air mail was flown by balloon from Lafayette, Indiana, in

162

1886. A mailbag containing circulars and letters was placed aboard the balloon at Lafayette. The balloon took off for New York City. It came down at Crawfordsville, twenty-seven miles away.

A unique claim put forward to justify McLeansboro's place in the sun was voiced by several different citizens.

"McLeansboro," they said, "is the only town in the entire United States that is named McLeansboro."

And not a single one of them mentioned Joe Allen's piano.

Chapter 13

Somewhere along the ragged line of my life I got joggled off the track and, instead of becoming a historian, found myself suddenly thrust into the unpleasant role of a philosopher. There was a turning point, but I have had difficulty locating it; it may have been the day when I summoned all my strength, picked up an Oliver typewriter, and threw it at my boss; or it may have been the time that managing editor in Louisville caught me in the act of doing a super-padding job on my expense account—a circumstance which led me to depart for Florida.

I have a talent for the kind of research that is necessary in the production of history books. Give me a stack of ancient newspaper files and I'll be a happy and contented human for hours. There in McLeansboro, Casey Dempsey had bound copies of the local papers dating back, it seemed, to the time of Amerigo Vespucci. It is a matter of regret to me that I could not tackle all of them—I had a date in St. Louis and I had to hurry things along. Being interested chiefly in myself, I picked out the files for 1905, 1906, and 1907. I wanted to find out what McLeansboro was like at, to me, its most splendid moment—the time of my birth.

The manner in which local happenings were reported in those days reminded me, somehow, of the newspapers in Great Britain today. British journalism, in fact, is a thing that has long been baffling to me. Some years ago I was on a radio program rigged up by the British Broadcasting Corporation. A rodeo cowboy named Homer Pettigrew, an actress named Janet Blair, and a comedian named Peter Donald sat with me in a New York studio. Across the water, in London, sat a rider-to-hounds, an English actress, an English comedian, and a guy who worked on a London newspaper. We were supposed to exchange ideas and opinions with one another, and when it came my turn I told the British journalist that he and his confreres of the London press needed very badly to learn how to write. He sputtered a little bit and then came out with, "Mr. Smith, you are a fool." That I didn't like—being called a fool on an international hookup, being called a fool across three thousand miles of deep water. So I told him he was a slob, and I was getting ready to reinforce that statement with more forceful language when Mr. Stephen Frye, who was running the show, hurled himself into the breach and got Homer Pettigrew to talking about how to rope a calf.

My friend Elmer Roessner was in England during the war and took pleasure in relaying British news items to me in New York. For example, he sent an item about Christopher Olsen, thirteen, of Southampton, who pointed a double-barreled shotgun through the kitchen door and pulled the trigger, "and the charge entered the chest of 18-year-old Dorothy Rose Stroud, who was cutting up beans. She was killed instantly." The headline on this item was: 13-YEAR-OLD BOY'S PRANK ON MAID.

Among the other British news items sent me by Mr. Roessner were these:

Arthur Pugg once hit 101 in 18 minutes off four overs (1 no ball) at Hastings.

Looking out to see the time, Mrs. Emily Brion, 81, of Eaton, fell from the window and died.

W. W. Bangs, who with Frank Young (Crouch Hill), won the Finchley Pairs Bowls Tournament, played in white flannels bought 42 years ago for 2s. 6d.

Peter Geeson, aged 15, has caught a 4 lb. 15 oz. tench at Tring.

Joe Davis once missed the reds altogether in his opening stroke at snooker at Thurston's. Cue-ball struck cushions seven times, and then struck black, a forfeit of seven points.

In the McLeansboro *Times* of forty years ago I found an item which said Judge C. B. Thomas had been boasting of the time he ran for county treasurer. "I was the only man," said Judge Thomas, "who was ever nominated by acclamation and unanimously defeated."

The country correspondence in those old papers, news from places such as Dog Town and Opossum Creek and Piopolis, was fully as interesting as the items pertaining to McLeansboro itself. Most of the country correspondents seemed to be temperance people, and the demon rum was roughed up in almost every column of crossroads chitchat. There were items such as this:

Ernest Bode was seen Saturday night riding his horse in Craw Lane. Drunk as usual.

Or this one:

The neighbors of Mrs. Katie Gregg saved her from being murdered last week when they found her husband beating her with a piece of stovewood. He has been drunk for three years.

Along about the time of my birth Mrs. Martha Gullic inserted an ad in the *Times*. It was strongly worded. Her husband, Theodore, had just died and she wanted to deny the malicious gossip that he passed away in consequence of drinking wood alcohol. It was nothing more, said his widow, than cramps of the stomach and bowels. Her notice was headed: Card of Thanks.

McLeansboro today is a comparatively wealthy town because of oil production. The oil fields of Hamilton County were first tapped around 1939, and at this writing there are more than eight hundred wells operating there, and a big refinery has been built just south of McLeansboro. As early as 1906, however, the people of McLeansboro were dazzled by the prospect of oil being found beneath their feet. The newspapers of that year contained much oil talk, items such as this: "A. C. Johnson has discovered oil in Crouch Township by using a magic wand cut off a peach tree." Almost every week, in fact, someone discovered oil, yet no oil was discovered. There is reason to suspect that dishonest people were loose in Egypt.

The big strike of those ancient times, however, came significantly during the very week of my birth in 1906. The local paper was almost raucous about it. Oil had been struck in General Campbell's cabbage patch and the hole had been stoppered with a four-foot ash plug. The editor of the *Times* screamed in print across the top of his front page:

"HURRAH! WE'LL ALL WEAR DIAMONDS!"

He was compelled to report in his next issue that the oil from General Campbell's cabbage patch had soon turned to salt water, and he was bitter about it and reported that it was common knowledge around town that the hole had been drilled in the cabbage patch and several barrels of imported oil had been poured into it.

The winter of 1906 was an unhappy one for McLeansboro over and above the cabbage-patch fraud. The *Times* reported that the streets were two feet deep in mud, a condition that brought on a minor coal famine. The mud was so deep that wagons couldn't get through it and coal had to be hauled in wheelbarrows or toted in tow sacks. Meanwhile my uncle Sam Allen was distinguishing himself in a debate held by the eighth-graders. The subject: Resolved, that fire has done more damage than water.

Then there was a sporting event with a British flavor—an account of a basketball game between the McLeansboro High School boys and a team called the Tigers. It was held in the county courtroom, rented for the occasion, and to this day nobody knows how it came out. The *Times* account said that "in the last quarter the referee and the timer got rattled and couldn't figure out what the score was so all bets were called off."

Still another school item, which I think somebody made up, told of how Tom Barker had pulled a girl's hair, whereupon the teacher ordered him to stay after school and write a composition of fifty words. Tom Barker's composition was as follows:

Jessie was fond of kittens. She saw one in the road and called, "Here, pussy, pussy, pussy, pussy, pussy, pussy, pussy, pussy, pussy, pussy, pussy, pussy, pussy, pussy, pussy, pussy,

pussy, pussy, pussy, pussy, pussy, pussy, pussy, pussy, pussy, pussy, pussy, pussy, pussy, pussy, pussy, pussy, pussy, pussy, pussy, pussy.

I know of no Thomas Barker in American literature, yet surely that boy grew up to become a writer. Perhaps he's in advertising.

The *Times* of my Eagle Brand days was militant editorially. There was a stout editorial blast against "weeping at weddings." Almost every week there was a long disquisition against the cigarette evil. And one caustic assault was aimed at the "Teddy-bear fad." Modern woman, said the editor, was making a silly fool of herself by taking to Teddy bears, carrying them with her wherever she journeyed, cuddling them in the streets and in the theaters—"a pathetic spectacle of perverted motherhood."

A McLeansboro news item of 1906: John Parmley and Wallace Meador had an altercation on the west side of the square. Parmley hit Meador in the face with a posthole digger, inflicting serious wounds.

In exploring those old papers I found two articles of more significance than the minor items already reported. One of these dealt with the death of a man who appeared to be McLeansboro's Number-One war hero. His name was Major John B. Smith, no kin of mine, and he was eighty-eight when he died. His reputation as a hero was great, and was based on a single exploit—perhaps the most negative example of heroism in history. Much newspaper space was given over to his obituary and glowing tribute was paid to his heroic adventure.

He had served in both the Mexican and the Civil wars, but it was in the Mexican War that he made his reputation. The heroic act of Major Smith was this: he could have captured Santa Ana's cork leg at the Battle of Cerro Gordo in 1847 if he had wanted to, but he didn't want to.

A God's fact! The *Times* recounted the whole story in great detail. Along toward the end of the Battle of Cerro Gordo, Major Smith was pursuing the enemy. Shagging Mexicans across the fields, he suddenly came upon a splendid buggy that had been abandoned by the foe. He looked inside the buggy and saw a cork leg. He picked it up and handled it. He debated with himself whether he should capture it or whether he should leave it lay and go on chasing the enemy. At length he decided on the latter course.

So what happened after that? Along came a mere private named Abel Waldron. He, too, saw the buggy and found the leg and had the same debate with himself; but he came to a different decision and captured the leg. He brought it back in triumph—Santa Ana's very own cork leg. He was officially declared to be the captor of the leg and was saluted and honored as such. The leg itself was exhibited for a while at the United States Patent Office in Washington. Then, according to the *Times* account, it was taken to Springfield and placed "among the war relics of which Illinois is justly proud."

Three full columns were devoted to Major Smith's story and the injustice under which he suffered. The major was a modest man, however, and never let it be suspected that he was angry at Abel Waldron or the government of the United States. He, after all, was the true hero. He *could* have captured that leg. He was the first one to get there. He had *handled* it. He would not have been censured had he forgotten about the retreating Mexicans and contented himself with taking that leg prisoner. But he saw a higher duty, and eschewed the certain glory that would have been his had he captured the leg, and lit out after those Mexicans again.

The second *Times* article which attracted my attention concerned a certain Professor Oldreive and touches on me personally, in the same way that Santa Ana's leg touched on Major Smith personally. At the very moment of my birth Professor Oldreive was walking on water not many miles to the south of McLeansboro. The professor got into an argument with a steamboat captain in Cincinnati, claiming that he not only could walk on water but he could walk on water all the way from Cincinnati to New Orleans. The steamboat captain bet the professor five thousand dollars that he couldn't do it. Before long the professor was on his way, and he was walking on the surface of the Ohio River, passing Egypt, at the time I was born.

The dispatch to the *Times* said that Professor Oldreive wore shoes shaped like little boats. They were four feet long, six inches wide, and six inches deep. "At the bottom of each shoe," said the dispatch, "are duck flaps to aid the professor in moving forward."

Accompanying the professor on his long liquid walk were his wife and his manager, who traveled alongside him in a skiff. He walked "with a twisting motion," and progress was very slow because even the duck flaps wouldn't hold the shoes steady in water. The *Times* correspondent reported that there was much talk among the river-front Egyptians to the effect that the professor was a fake and that there was some kind of crooked business involved in his adventure. There was even gossip that he walked on water only when he was passing a town and that he rode in the skiff between towns. This allegation was hotly denied by the professor.

I have spent hours trying to find out if the professor ever made it, but I find no reference to him in the books I've examined. I doubt very much if he got to New Orleans, or even to Memphis. If, at any time in our history, a man walked on water from Cincinnati to New Orleans, and finished the journey, then he would certainly be in the history books, and there would be a statue of him, duck flaps and all, somewhere along the line.

Chapter 14

My aunt Vieve (short for Genevieve) is my father's sister and lives in a trim bungalow on North Washington Street, and when the time came for me to involve myself in some family history I consulted her, for she seems to be the nearest thing to a clan historian that we have. She got out some albums and I went through them. They were filled with ancient photographs, mostly of men with long beards and a belligerent fear of God reflected in their eyes; they all looked as though they hated the photographer who was taking their pictures and would shortly assault him. Most of them were my kin, but I had never heard of them and was just as happy that I hadn't. Those fierce-looking old baboons were inhabitants of Egypt and other parts of Illinois, and I can't understand why William Jennings Bryan, who must have grown up among them, ever went to Dayton, Tennessee, and took the side he did. The tintypes of my ancestors argue more for the theory of evolution than all the writings of Darwin.

Aunt Vieve also had scrapbooks, and these were intended originally as repositories for scraps of family history—newspaper clippings of births and marriages and who went to visit for a week in East St. Louis or Decatur. There were occasional items relating that Miss Genevieve Smith had gone to Decatur to visit relatives.

"Oh yes," said Aunt Vieve, "I used to be on the go all the time. I always went up to Decatur to visit the Skelleys, but every time I came back to McLeansboro, I'd swear I'd never do it again. In those days I thought the Skelley girls led an awful fast life. It was just go, go, go, go, from morning to night."

"Where did you go?" I asked her.

"Down to the drugstore," said Aunt Vieve. The memory of those days of helling around in a drugstore reminded her of some girls who were her friends in McLeansboro and whose father was a stern and righteous man. He was forever complaining to anyone who would listen about the corrupt ways of his girls. "All my daughters ever do," he would say, "is put talsum on their faces and go down to the depot."

Aunt Vieve grew up on the Home Place and stayed there after all the other children had married and moved away, stayed behind with the old folks until they were gone. She showed me Grandpa Caleb Smith's obituary and pointed out a line in which my grandparents were credited with having "reared to man and womanhood a family of most estimable children."

"That," said Aunt Vieve, "means everybody except your dad. Your grandmother was probably the most intelligent woman in Egypt, maybe even in Illinois, and had the strongest will of anybody I've ever known, but she could never do anything with your dad. What do you suppose is the matter with him?"

"That's easy," I told her. "He takes after me."

Aunt Vieve sold the Home Place in the 1920s and took quarters in a more centrally located part of town. At that time there was an elderly farmer, a bachelor, living a few miles from McLeansboro. He had been trying, for something like thirty years, to bag a wife. He kept tabs on vital statistics in McLeansboro; the moment a woman, any woman, became a widow, he got out his razor and shaved himself and before long he would arrive in his surrey with a proposal of marriage. He kept himself informed on the romantic affairs of every maiden lady in town, and on hearing that a girl had quarreled with her boy friend, he would dash into town and ask her for her hand. Nobody would have him, but he didn't give up.

Aunt Vieve was getting along toward fifty when she moved into town and had never been married. The day following her arrival in her new quarters the wife-hunter was at her door. She told him no, and he got down on his knees and clasped his hands together and begged her to be his wife. She still said no. He considered this stout refusal for a few moments, then played his trump card.

"Miss Genevieve," he said, "I'll tell you what. If you'll marry me *I'll buy you a Shetland pony!*"

Somehow the offer didn't appeal to her and she sent him away. So far as she knows, the poor fellow never did get a wife, with or without his offer of lagniappe.

I was all ready to start for the Home Place, but a telephone call came from a Mrs. Green. She said that her late husband had been a friend of Grandpa Cad Allen and that Grandpa Allen had once presented Mr. Green with a very famous meerschaum pipe. Now that Mr. Green was gone, said his widow, I could have that famous pipe if I wanted it. I am not a smoker of pipes, nor a collector of antiques, but I hurried over to Mrs. Green's house. I asked her what was famous about the pipe, and she said that it had once belonged to Captain Longworth and that Captain Longworth had been an admirer of my grandfather and had given it to him, and my grandfather had been an admirer of Mr. Green and had given it to *him*. She went into another room and got out the pipe, which looked somewhat like a small saxophone and had a nice balance to it when you hefted it, so that if you got a good grip on the stem you could kill a man with it.

My main interest was in the historical significance of this pipe, and I asked Mrs. Green about the Captain Longworth who had given it to my grandfather.

"You mean to sit there and say you never heard of Captain Longworth?" she said. "Why, he was famous around here."

"What was he famous for?"

"Well, I couldn't say for sure, but anybody in McLeansboro will tell you he was famous. I think he must have been in some war or other. You look up about him and you'll find that that pipe is about as famous a pipe as there is in the country."

I went back to the house where I was rooming and cross-examined Orlin Davis, the former James Whitcomb Riley reader and flat-foot waltzer. I asked him if he had known Captain Longworth.

"Yes," said Mr. Davis, "I remember him. I think he clerked in a grocery store. He wasn't around here very long."

"What was he famous for?"

"He wasn't famous for anything that I ever heard about. He just clerked in a grocery store."

"Why was he called 'Captain'?"

"Because he was a private in the Civil War."

I started back for Aunt Vieve's house, but Mr. Davis called after me and I returned to the porch swing.

"I've been hearing about the books you write," he said with a sly look. "I hear," he went on, dropping his voice to a whisper, "that they're a little risky."

"That's what some people say."

So he told me a "risky" story of his own which he said he had heard once in Chicago. It didn't seem risky to me, but then maybe my sense of riskiness has been warped through years of living in New York.

I took Private Longworth's pipe and went along to Aunt Vieve's and found her reading the *Times-Leader,* and something in its pages was causing her to giggle one moment and express indignation the next. She showed me a one-column ad in the paper. Here it is:

NOTICE!
As I am Mayor of Persimmon Ridge, I will buy, sell, or trade for anything from a six-cylinder Tom cat to a twenty-seven-striped Zebra.

Come out for oil stoves and used furniture.

D. N. Alley

Mayor of Persimmon Ridge

One block north of Davis' Laundry.

"Darn him, anyway," said Aunt Vieve.

"Who is he?"

"He's the one," she said, "who owns the Home Place now.

And look what he's calling it! Persimmon Ridge! Some of the family still own some lots out there, and he's been running these ads lately and always calling it Persimmon Ridge. Just as sure as you're born that name will stick, and it'll always be known as Persimmon Ridge, and laughed at, and that property won't be worth a dime. What makes me so mad is that there's not a persimmon tree in a mile of the Home Place, and I ought to know. Darn him!"

Aunt Vieve had never once been back to the Home Place since the day she sold it, and when I asked her to accompany me she was almost as eager for the visit as I was. We drove over and picked up Aunt Nellie Hassett, who also grew up on the Home Place, and her daughter Veronica, and headed for Persimmon Ridge.

Mr. D. N. Alley greeted us with a brisk cordiality, wearing overalls and a railroader's cap. He was a little, fast-talking, energetic man, and he told me he had retired from railroading.

The Home Place is a small one-story house shaped like a salt box and surrounded by ancient trees, none of which produce persimmons. My two aunts were pleased to see that the mayor of Persimmon Ridge was keeping it in excellent shape. The grass was cut and the shrubs trimmed and flowers were growing all over the place. Mr. Alley took us into the house and showed us from room to room and pointed out little improvements he had made and others he contemplated making. It was a wonderful occasion for Aunt Vieve and Aunt Nellie, for they hadn't been inside that house in twenty years. Aunt Nellie, who is seventy-seven and very tiny, called me into the kitchen and showed me a window.

"Did you ever hear," she said, "about the time I whipped the rooster?" I hadn't, and she told me about it. She had been baking cherry pies, and when she took them out of the oven she set them on the window sill to cool. Half an hour later she walked into the kitchen and found a rooster on the sill, pecking away at the pies. She was understandably furious. She knew nothing of the accepted manner in which chickens should be punished, if there was an accepted manner. She knew of only one way to punish a miscreant—

the method favored by humans. She ran out into the yard, cut herself a switch from a tree, and started chasing that rooster, and whenever she'd get in range she'd give him a cut across the bottom.

"Everybody laughed at me," she said, "but I tell you one thing—that rooster never touched another one of my pies."

In the little dining room Aunt Vieve remembered something about my father.

"He always liked to drink," she said, "even when he was around sixteen or seventeen. Your grandfather usually kept a bottle of whisky around the house to use for medicine, and we had trouble hiding it from your dad. There was a couch right around the corner there, in the living room, and one day we tucked the whisky bottle down behind the pillows. That afternoon your dad came in and stretched himself out on the couch for a nap. Your grandmother and I were working at something here in the dining room, sitting at the table. We couldn't see Harry, but we knew he was there on the couch and that the bottle was within inches of him and he didn't know it. It just tickled us silly to think about it. We whispered and giggled over it and we could hear him snoring a little. We thought it was a great joke on him till he finally got up and came staggering into this room, and we rushed in and found the bottle empty. He had been lying there all the time, faking sleep, making out that he was snoring, and while we were whispering and giggling he had finished off that bottle and got as tight as a hoot owl."

Opposite the kitchen door of the little house stands a one-room shed. Caleb Smith was proprietor of a prosperous brickyard on the land just north of the house, but originally he had been a cigar maker and he continued to make cigars for himself and his friends throughout his life. The little shed was his private cigar factory, and in it Caleb had taught my father how to roll and wrap cigars.

In the early years of his marriage Pop was strawboss at the brickyard, but along about 1912 or 1913 the brick business hit a bad slump, and that's when he took his family north to Decatur, where he went to work as a cigar maker.

It was an interesting sort of job, the way Pop tells about it. There were sixteen men working at tables in a big room.

Among them would be several hobo cigar makers, men who were spiritually kin to the old-time tramp newspapermen. Each man had a sort of rating. The most expert were rated at five hundred cigars a day. Each cigar maker, especially the five-hundred-a-day men, developed little tricks for the purpose of eliminating waste motion and speeding up his personal production. If a man was a five-hundred-a-day cigar maker, he was his own boss so long as he turned out those five hundred. The same was true of a two-hundred-a-day man, which was Pop's rating. If he could manage to turn out his two hundred cigars by midafternoon, he could knock off for the remainder of the day; no more was expected of him, no more was wanted of him. The experts had a keen sense of timing; they worked with their watches hung on a nail in front of them and they knew just where they should be at any given minute of the day. Most of them enjoyed drinking, and it was common practice for a cigar maker to work furiously for several hours in order to get, say, twenty or thirty minutes ahead of his own schedule, at which point he'd drop everything, slap on his hat, and head for a saloon. He knew exactly how long he could be away from his bench and the exact minute when he would have to resume putting Little Roses together. That was the brand Pop made, and the brand Old Caleb made in the same shop, forty years before him.

These Illinois cigar makers had no reader, that being strictly a Latin-American institution. In Cuba and other Latin countries where cigars are made, and in Tampa where the cigar makers are Latins, a man is employed and paid by the workers to sit at one end of the room and read aloud throughout the day.

"Up North," Pop told me, "we never had a reader, but we had a system of talkin'. We had one guy named Benny, and ever' morning after we'd got into the swing of the work, somebody would yell out, 'Start somethin', Benny.' That meant Benny was to think up a good subject to talk about. In a little while Benny would say, maybe, 'Airplanes.' Then the guy on the end next to the door would start to talk. He'd talk about airplanes. Maybe he'd say that by God they'd never git *him* up in one of them things. He'd tell

SMOKE SMITH'S
★ LITTLE ROSES ★

about the first time he'd ever seen one. And he'd say if God meant fer us to fly he'd-a put feathers on us. When he got through it moved on to the next man and he would talk as long as he could about airplanes and it would go all around the room like that. The only one that never talked on any of the subjects was Benny. He was good at pickin' subjects—he was always the one that picked out the subject—but he couldn't talk about anything worth a damn, and didn't want to.

"I remember once when Benny give us the subject about plantin' crops in the light of the moon or the dark of the moon. Ever'body had a strong opinion; me and one other fella, we were the only ones that said we didn't believe in that crap. You never heard such argyin'! It almost ended up in a fight. Finely ever'body decided they would appoint me to write a letter to the State Agriculture Department in Springfield and git a scientific answer to it. We wanted to have it settled once and fer all. So I wrote to the head guy of the Agriculture Department and in about a week I got my answer. That son-of-a-bitch was a politician and hedged on me. He wrote this letter and said in it, 'I have no official data on this matter. Some people say the moon affects plantings and other people say it don't. It is my personal opinion, however, that there may be something to it, although it might be that there is nothing to it.' I could tell in a minute that he was gettin' ready to run for governor or somethin' and he wasn't gonna take a chance on losin' any votes by comin' out one way or another about the moon. I'm glad it happened the way it did because it woke me up to these politicians. I got no use for the bastards. Why couldn't he come right out and take a stand on this moon business? He knew damn well that the moon's got nothin' to do with plantin' reddishes or corn or when you should put shingles on your house. But would he say so? No!"

We looked into the shed where Pop learned to make cigars, but there wasn't even a tobacco smell left in it. The mayor of Persimmon Ridge, as I've suggested, was extremely hospitable to his visitors and realized that there was a lot of sentiment attached to our call and had no trouble getting himself into the proper mood for the occasion. After we had all got back into the car he came over and stood by the window and asked me if I was going back to New York. When I said I was, he thought for a moment, then said:

"When you get back to New York, you go down and see the mayor of New York, and you tell him the mayor of Persimmon Ridge sends greetings to the mayor of New York. Will you do 'er?"

"Certainly," I told him.

He must have figured that I was bursting with nostalgia during my visit to Persimmon Ridge, because a week or so after I left town he turned up at the Hassett house with a handwritten poem. He asked that it be forwarded to me, which it was. I am against permitting poetry to insinuate itself into my books except when written by Gene Fowler, but this particular poem is so touching and reverent that I think I'll include it. Here it is just as the poet set it down:

OUR VISITORS

There were some folks came to our house the other day,
And said they were from New York, and that is far away,
He told me his name, "Smith" he said
I lived here when a boy, with my Dad and Aunty there,
And some times, she would give me an awful scare.
He spoke about my self claimed fame as Mayor of Persimmon
    Ridge.
Little did I know I was talking to a Famed Poet, or writer,
    should I say,
I just tried to make his visit pleasant,
For to visit the Old Home is something really grand,
He took some pictures and looked all about
While there was that look of something that was left out,
Now Mr. Smith, I know just what it is,
For when I go back to my old home,
It isn't as it was, we miss Those dear ones who have left us,
We can't forget them and no others will we ever find to take
    their place, and with us be so kind,
They seemed to know and somehow understand
Just when a fellow would need a friend.
Since God has taken them away and we have no one to tell us
    how to go,
Here is what I try to do, I try to follow as they would have
    me go,

So when *The Father* calls me,
I can go and meet them and receive a *Welcome Home.*
                    —*written by* BILL THE BUM

I don't know why he put that signature at the end. Humorous touch, probably.

Chapter 15

It is required by law that any person who undertakes a reminiscence of childhood in the Midwest shall write at least one chapter, and preferably eight, about food. It is not necessary that he deal with the taste of it, the smell of it being more important. Unfortunately, I can remember only one fact about food as it touched my consciousness during the first six years of my life. Bacon rind was always saved and put aside in our house and my father used it to rub on his handsaw.

Eating habits have not changed much in McLeansboro down through the years, I was told, and I can report that the people were great eaters in 1906 as they are in 1947. They stack it high, and anything that can be fried, they fry it. That is why, even in the enlightened age of the atomic bomb, I often defy my wife, who is a broiler, and fry stuff for myself. She believes, with a great many other people, that fried foods are all but lethal. I once tried to convince her of her error by showing her a public statement made by Satchel Paige, the great Negro pitcher, who attributed his strength and stamina to the fact that he eats nothing unless it is fried. It didn't work; she doesn't understand baseball.

Dinner is at noon in McLeansboro, but that fact does not necessarily suggest provincialism. I live within commuting distance of New York City, and recently I invited a couple from Chappaqua to drive over to a fancy roadhouse in Connecticut for dinner the following day. My guests were natives of Chappaqua and are reckoned to be quite civilized and urbane. They were to drive to my house and we would go on to Connecticut in my car, but no hour was mentioned—I assumed that they would know enough to arrive around six-thirty or seven. They came at 11:45 A.M., at which time I was gutting a shad, and when I was unable to conceal my surprise they remarked, "You said dinner, didn't you?" My years of high living in New York City have made me enough of a snob to eat dinner in the evening, though I escaped the metropolis before catching the plague which causes people like Chicago-born and Brooklyn-reared Dorothy Kilgallen to say "Notruh Domm" and "eyether" and "nyether."

At the home of the Cooneys, who are cousins, we had a magnificent meal one noontime—fried chicken, fried potatoes, fried lettuce, fried peas, fried lemon-chiffon pie, and coffee that was first put through the percolator and then, I think, fried. Most of my McLeansboro relatives were present for this banquet, and while we sopped gravy I brought up the matter of my actual birthplace.

Aunt Nellie, with the wisdom of her years, said I was born in the little house on Hancock Street. Her daughter, Eula Cooney, said she didn't think so; that she seemed to remember that the Smiths moved to another little house about a block from the Catholic church just before I was born. Aunt Vieve was under the impression that we already lived in the house on East Main Street, next door to Hat Goodrich. Aunt Nellie insisted that she ought to know the circumstances of the mighty event—her husband was the attending physician at my birth, and they, the Hassetts, lived catty-cornered across the street from the house on Hancock Street. Veronica Hassett said she was too young to remember, but that there were plenty of people in town who would know for certain and she'd instigate an investigation at once. As soon as she found out which house was the correct one, she said, she would get some film and take some pictures of me in front of my birthplace . . . for posterity and the local newspaper.

At the Cooney fry Aunt Nellie told about Dicker and Valentine—bachelor brothers to my Grandpa Smith. These two lived in a little cottage next door to the Home Place. They seldom went into the business district unless their brother Caleb was going. He, my grandfather, was about five feet tall; Dicker was a little taller, and Valentine was the tallest of the three. It was their custom always to walk in single file wherever they went—Caleb in front, then Dicker, and Valentine bringing up the rear. That's the way they always traveled, and as the small parade moved from the Home Place to the square they rarely spoke a word to each other. It was a common remark among the towns-people, when they saw the Smith men approaching, to say: "Well, here comes rag, tag, and bobtail." I am a grandson of Rag.

I have no memory of these two great-uncles, for which I'm sorry, because they were characters of considerable color. Dicker, for example, was a colossal skeptic and muttered constantly against the automobile after its arrival on the streets of McLeansboro. He called the new machines "mottomobiles," and his constant plaint, 'to anyone who would listen, was: "Mottomobiles is ruinin' th' country." Toward the close of his life the first radio receiving sets were introduced into McLeansboro. He was invincible in his refusal to believe in radio. They almost had to hog-tie him the one time they managed to get a set of earphones on his head. He listened just a few seconds, then ripped the head-set off and dashed it to the floor. It was a dirty fake, he said, and he continued saying that till he died.

None of my relatives remembered anything about the matter of me and the comet pills. That was a story my father told me not long ago, saying that he had kept it a secret for years because he had certain fears about it.

Back about 1910, on a Saturday afternoon, Pop and some of his friends took what he calls a kag of beer into the woods. They set the kag on a hillside and went to work on it with no thought for sprites or elves or nymphs, and when they had finished it they returned to town and found a pitchman from St. Louis at work on the courthouse square. This man had come into McLeansboro with a barrel (or kag) full of pills.

Halley's comet was in the sky at that time, and the pitchman preached that the comet was giving off lethal gases, that a mere whiff of these fumes would be sufficient to kill a person, and that the only way to gain immunity from death by comet gas was to swallow one of his pills. They were twenty-five cents each, and the man was selling them as fast as he could hand them out. Word of his presence, and of his lifesaving pills, spread swiftly over the county, and those farmers not already in town were hitching up their sandy-land mules and hurrying across the dusty roads, hoping the comet gas wouldn't get them before they reached the square.

My father said he listened to the pitchman's spiel and, becoming smitten with beery foreboding, got to worrying about me, his only son, and the likelihood of my being carried off by comet fumes before I'd even had a good start in life; so he quietly bought one of the pills and hurried home with it, and when nobody was looking poked it down my gullet. Right after that I got the croup and diphtheria, but Pop said he doesn't think the comet pill was responsible.

"I never told anybody about it," he said, "because I figured maybe that pill was the thing that made you turn out bad."

I am unable to convey, in print, the nuances he managed to get into that last statement, but his manner and tone indicated clearly that I suffer from a virulent form of insanity and he hopes to God he is not to blame for it.

As I said, none of my relatives could remember this incident, though somebody did recollect that there was a Halley's comet around 1910. So we finished the big dinner and then went out to lie on the grass and pant and groan.

Meanwhile quite a few McLeansboro citizens were keeping the telephones ringing in the homes of my kinfolks. During the time I was in town three different men telephoned and said the same thing, almost in the same words: "Hell, you oughta remember *me*. I'm the one pulled you out of that cistern you fell in." Later on, when I told my father about this, he said that all three of them were liars, that he himself pulled me out.

A woman whose name I neglected to get called to report an incident which she said occurred when I was about four years old. She was, at that time, a neighbor of ours, and she said I turned up at her house one afternoon and said:

"Odie, give me some tobacco."

"What on earth do you want with tobacco?" she demanded.

"I'm gonna chew," I said, "and then I'm gonna SPIT!"

Somewhere along in here Doc Tevis telephoned Veronica Hassett and told her he had been a pal of my father's when they were young men and he would greatly enjoy having a talk with me. He was a dentist, so I arranged to have him clean my teeth while he told me stories of old times in McLeansboro. He had a machine going inside my mouth as he talked and I couldn't take notes, but I remember some of the things he talked about.

During one of the brief periods when McLeansboro tolerated saloons, a man named Earl Something kept a bar on the square. His best customer was a middle-aged citizen, a retired farmer, who was a sort of marathon drinker. This man was always waiting at the door each morning when Earl arrived to open the saloon. The customer began his day with breakfast—three quick ones. Then he walked out and took his place at the curb, leaning against one of the iron posts which supported the shed roof over the sidewalk. He would lean there motionless for perhaps an hour, then march back into the saloon, have another drink, and return to his pole. This procedure was repeated during all the hours the saloon was open.

One morning he must have had an upset stomach; either that or he took on more than his customary load. At any rate, he was leaning against his pole along about noontime when his legs collapsed and he slumped to the curb and just lay there. A few moments later a prominent merchant came down the sidewalk. He took one look at the fallen man, stepped over to the door of the saloon, stuck his head inside, and yelled:

"Hey, Earl! Yer sign's down!"

I asked Doc Tevis if the town had a village atheist, which is standard equipment for small communities, and he said

186

he didn't believe so at the moment; but at one time there was an old guy who went around talking socialism and atheism and, as regards the latter creed, had a convincer which he used on anybody who would hear him out. After enumerating all the standard proofs, McLeansboro's village atheist would deliver his convincer as follows:

"You think they's a God? You think they's a God that's alwees good to his childern? Well, I'll show you how good he is. You ever look at a hawg real close? How many hams has he got on him? Right. Two hams. On the back. Now —WHY AIN'T HE ALSO GOT HAMS ON THE FRONT? If they was a God, that space on the front of a hawg wouldn't of been wasted, would it? They ain't no reason on earth why a hawg shouldn't pervide a man with four hams steada two, and if they was a God and he was takin' care uh his childern, then by God he'd-a put them exter hams on."

Doc Tevis finished mining the slag off my teeth, hung up his drill, then stood back and looked at me as I lay in his chair. Finally he grinned a broad grin, and then he started whacking me across the nose with his index finger, roaring:

"Right, by God, on the end of your nose, you look exactly like your old man!"

The resemblance has been remarked by other people; my father and I have double-ended noses.

And when I tried to pay him for the teeth-cleaning, he almost threw a fit.

"Not a penny!" he announced. "That job's on old Harry, God love 'im!"

Back at Aunt Vieve's house the telephone was still ringing. Mrs. Madaline Mattingly, the librarian, had arranged a reception for us at the Public Library the next evening. Aunt Nellie had called to say that she had talked to a woman who knew all about the circumstances of my birth. This woman said I was born in the house on Hancock Street —that she was positive about it because she had gone over to the house that evening to take charge of my two sisters.

Aunt Vieve would not be convinced on the strength of this woman's story and suggested that further investigation was in order. Aunt Nellie said she thought Aunt Vieve was being unreasonable, but Aunt Vieve stuck to her guns. Cousin Veronica set out again to seek additional evidence. As for me, I was not greatly concerned—I figured they'd finally get the correct house. By this time, and in spite of the nearness of John Stelle Day—the greatest day in McLeansboro history—half the town appeared to be in a high sweat over getting my birthplace properly located.

The reception at the library had some sentimental value to it because the building was made out of bricks baked by my grandfather. It was the first such social function I had ever attended, and my wife had to instruct me in protocol. We stood just inside the entrance to the library, with Aunt Vieve and Mrs. Mattingly running interference. As each person came in he or she got the once-over from Mrs. Mattingly, who passed each customer along to Aunt Vieve, who introduced my wife and then me.

After maybe fifty people had run the gantlet we broke up the reception line and I started signing autographs. In all that crowd, however, there was only one person who brought along one of my books to be autographed. He was a boy of high-school age, full of electricity and vinegar. We went over to a table in the children's department and I set to work with the inscription. He spread his elbows out on the table like a rooster flexing his wing muscles, and when I had finished the autographing he said with passion:

"Now. What's your opinion of poetry?"

Almost exactly as I had performed in the presence of Dr. Will Durant back in Denver.

"What do you mean?" I said uneasily. I could see that he was prepared, maybe even rehearsed, for an extensive discussion of poetry, and I knew that in his pocket were poems of his own devising and that he was going to spring them on me. This I could do without.

"You like it, don't you—poetry?" he said.

"God, no!" I said with fervor. "I hate it!" I left him sitting there slack-jawed, and I think he departed soon after that —probably went home and burned the autographed book.

I signed my name twenty or thirty times that evening, but only that one time in a book. The ladies of McLeansboro

are collectors of autographed handkerchiefs. They came carrying silk handkerchiefs and they lined up and presented them to me and I did the best I could under the circumstances. I had finished off all the handkerchiefs when a matronly lady came up to me and asked me if I would autograph her dress. She indicated two strips of cloth which came down from her throat and dangled over her chest— I suppose you'd call it a tie.

She was a fine-looking woman with a fine figure, and I wanted to oblige her but I didn't quite know how to go about it. I came up close to her and scrutinized the tie and even felt of it, and told her that if I wrote on that cloth with a pen I'd ruin her dress—the ink would smear all over everything.

"Oh, no it won't!" she assured me. "And anyway, I want you to do it—I'd just *love* to have your autograph on here."

I took my fountain pen in hand and then reached for the two strands of the tie and tried to figure a way of doing it gracefully. There were lots of people looking on, and I got a slight case of panic when I realized that the only practical method of autographing the tie would be to press it down against her breast, twist myself into a sort of horizontal position, and write. As long as I had to do it that way—as long as the lady was asking for it—I decided to use the style of penmanship I learned long ago in school: rest the muscles of the forearm on the desk (chest, in this case) and go into extensive revolving motions to form the letters. This was going to be awful, but pleasant. I took hold of the tie with my left hand and let my right hand, carrying the pen, approach that fine writing surface. Nervously I glanced up, and there stood County Judge Eckley, and beside him was Com Wright, and next to Com Wright was mine host Orlin Davis, all of them watching every move I made.

A few feet away stood a bookcase, chest high and with a flat top. I took hold of the lady's tie and gingerly pulled her over to the bookcase, and laid the tie flat on the top of it and quickly signed my name. The ink made a frightful smear, and the thing that was supposed to be my signature would never be honored at my bank, but I was happy to get it over, and the lady said it was wonderful and she'd never wash that tie as long as she lived, and I headed for the punch bowl. I found it to be full of punch. Fruit punch. Meaning it was made from the juices of fruit and nothing else. So we sat around in a big room, and an eighty-four-year-old woman (I believe her name was Mrs. Utley) said she knew my grandparents and my great-grandparents and told me about them at great length, although someone else said later that Mrs. Utley had everything all mixed up, being so old and all. And Mrs. Mattingly got out her manuscript for me to read—it was *Romeo and Juliet* done in modern slang—and I said I thought it was *very* good, and Com Wright, who runs the hotel, wanted to know how my aunt Tyrrell was, and Bertha Woodruff, who had come over from Benton for John Stelle Day, said she remembered me when I was a baby and that I was purty. Over in a corner I found Aunt Vieve having a spirited conversation with several women concerning the search for the house in which I was born. Nothing definite came of it, though two or three of the women had strong opinions on the matter, so we all got out of there and went home.

Chapter 16

The following day we arose early in the home of Orlin Davis, and my wife remarked that my heart seemed to be young and gay, more so than usual.

"Don't you realize," I said, "that this is the day I stand before the humble cottage in which I was born?"

"Yes," she said, "I realize it. Have I heard anything else for the last week? I wish to God you'd forget about it and stop all this inane jabber about it. Who do you think you are —Voltaire?"

"In the first place," I said, "I haven't been jabbering about it. All these other people have been doing the jabbering. And in the second place, if that's the way you feel about it, you can go somewhere and fry yourself a meal and I'll handle this thing alone. I don't care if you *never* see the place where I was born."

Up to that moment she had taken McLeansboro without complaining, but I knew portions of it had been rough on her. The dust, for one thing. In Egypt we had not seen any of that mud which Dickens and Ingersoll had found to be the chief characteristic of the region. I don't, however, believe I was ever in a dustier place. The stuff seemed to hang suspended in the air and moved around only when it wanted to get into the houses or into my nostrils. For a while I was puzzled by the presence of all this dust, but then I figured it out. Egypt still has its mud in rainy spells, and when the farmers come into town the stuff accumulates on the wheels of their cars and wagons and is deposited on the pavements of the county seat where, in time, it becomes dust. The process is known as chemical engineering, and my son will be proud of me for having doped it out. A McLeansboro housewife can mop and wipe and scour furiously from one end of her home to the other, and by the time she reaches the kitchen it would be possible for her to go back into the living room and write a symphony on top of the piano with her finger. I must confess that I hated that dust as much as my wife hated it, but I think it's a small quibble, and if I had lived all of my forty years in McLeansboro, I might possibly have got accustomed to it by this time, and I would have been uncomfortable and asthmatic without it.

I went over to Aunt Vieve's house and found her answering phone calls, most of them concerned with the big birthplace argument. One call, however, came from the Pemberton boys. How the honors poured in upon me! The Pemberton boys said they would consider it a high compliment if I would visit their shirt factory, which was just across the street. I was in no mood to visit a shirt factory, until I remembered the sign on the building. The shirts that were made there were called Mark Twain shirts, and I'm a sucker for anything with the name Mark Twain on it.

The Pemberton boys took me through, starting in the basement and following the shirt assembly line to the top floor. The place was jammed with women and girls, and I found three more of my relatives working on the assembly line—relatives I hadn't met up to then. One of them was my cousin Irene, who is a trifle older than me, and I asked her if she remembered anything about the place where I was born. She said she certainly did, and I suggested that she get together with Aunt Vieve and Aunt Nellie at lunchtime (dinnertime) and see if she couldn't help straighten matters out.

At the time I was in McLeansboro one of the most talked-about shortages in the American economy was the shortage of white shirts. When the Pemberton boys got me to the end of the production line they presented me with two

Mark Twain shirts, both white. I was happy to get them simply because there was a white-shirt shortage; I didn't see any reason to tell the Pemberton boys that I quit wearing white shirts years ago, preferring thousand-milers which I can wear for a week without their showing the dirt—even for two or three weeks when there's nobody around with sensitive nostrils.

Back at Aunt Vieve's we got to talking about the remarkable character who was my grandmother Smith—the woman who fouled up my birth records and, in doing it, gave me a case of jitters long years after her death. Aunt Vieve told me how one of the first telephones in McLeansboro was installed at the Home Place, and how, whenever it rang, Grandma Smith would run her tongue over her lips and smooth down her hair before answering it. And how she argued Grandpa Smith out of the Republican party and into the Democratic—a feat which I was given to understand was a classic of polemical suasion. And how she was darn near an aristocrat, having been the granddaughter of a man who was landscape gardener on the estate of Henry Clay at Versailles, Kentucky.

This discussion made it absolutely necessary that I go out to the cemetery and see the graves of Caleb and Beatrice Smith. Among the many obsessions which weigh upon me is one involving cemeteries; I am allergic to them, and to funerals. But in the face of all the kindness that had been shown me, I couldn't refuse to make this pilgrimage, and so we went out and read headstones.

My attitude toward funerals and graveyards puts me in a minority, I know, but I am certainly not alone; many persons of my acquaintance share it, and among them is my friend Ben Serkowich. I treasure a copy of a letter he once wrote to the proprietor of a big New York cemetery. Some jocund pal had handed in Ben's name and he was placed on the cemetery's mailing list, and thereafter he began receiving goofy literature, urging him to grab himself some ground before the prices went up, which they were going to do, and urging him to come out and note the spaciousness, beauty, and privacy that make each family plot a sanctuary. The graveyard literature, in fact, was so beautiful that it almost made a man want to drop whatever he was doing and rush out and embrace a typhoid carrier.

In time, however, the lovely language and the color photos began to get on Ben's nerves, and finally he sat down and wrote a letter to the cemetery's head man. Here it is:

DEAR SIR:

Will you please remove my name from your mailing list? Your frequent sales-campaign letters make me so nervous that I have learned to hate you.

I have evolved a scheme, therefore, completely eliminating any possibility of my ever being cemetery-buried. I am going to have myself wrapped in self-igniting ganz-schmaltz and dropped by parachute from an airplane two hundred miles at sea. This will obviate any possibility of profit to preachers, florists, tombstone peddlers, cemetery real-estate promoters, or paid mourners.

Furthermore, I am having this letter published in the hope that other harassed citizens will follow suit. Undoubtedly you have caused a great deal of anguish to others with your sales letters, and especially your "courtesy card," which you say entitles me to a choice location facing the Administration Building if mailed before July 18. I give you my solemn word of honor that:

(a) I will be out of town until September.

(b) I'm not ever going to be buried.

(c) If I were going to be buried, I wouldn't want to be buried facing any Administration Building because I hate Administration Buildings and Administrator-minded people, especially cemetery administrators.

Now that you know how I feel you will save postage and printing costs by removing my name from your sucker list. I don't know how I got on it in the first place, unless some mishumored friend did it; or perhaps you bought a name list from the Charity League.

In any event, there is no possibility of your ever getting me for a customer. Many people are afraid I am going to live forever on account of my utterly mean disposition. But in case of my demise, the Health Department has orders and funds to dispose of my carcass in the manner above described.

Sincerely,

BENJ. H. SERKOWICH

Maybe Ben was a little severe with the cemetery man, but I don't think so. Even as I write this an item appears in

Variety concerning an Irish tenor named Jimmy Lennon who left a radio program in Hollywood to become staff funeral-soloist under contract to a big mortuary outfit. The company maintains a list of songs which is handed to mourners, and the mourners pick out the songs they want this Jimmy Lennon to sing. According to the *Variety* item, the song pluggers of Hollywood have laid siege to the tenor, trying to get him to put their songs on the list. Moreover, says *Variety*, the pluggers were having success and Mr. Lennon had added two currently popular numbers, "To Each His Own" and "Peg o' My Heart," to the list.

As for myself, when temperate living catches up to me, I too have plans for disposition of my carcass. I have left explicit instructions that I am to be promptly cremated and my ashes are to be shot out of the gun they use to shoot puffed wheat out of.

After the visit to the cemetery came another chicken dinner, and after that considerable telephoning, and at last it was settled that I was born in the house on Hancock Street. There was no question about it now; the evidence was even convincing enough to win over Aunt Vieve, who had held out for a house up near the Cooney place.

Veronica arrived with her camera and the two of us set out for Christian Hill. This is the name given the eastern residential section of the town as opposed to Dogtown on the west. If I had been given my choice, I think I would have chosen Dogtown as my favorite place to be born, just so I could talk about it, but it was Christian Hill and Hancock Street. We pulled up in front of the little white cottage and Veronica said: "There she is."

"Bow your head," I said. "Always be reverent in front of this house."

"Okay," said Veronica. "Now get over there in the yard and pose."

"Maybe the people who live here won't like it."

Veronica said she didn't know who lived in the house, but she felt certain that nobody could object to my having a picture taken in front of it. I got out and walked across the scraggy lawn, deep in thought, searching my soul for a tingle, a stab of pain, a stone, a leaf, an unfound door. There was a door leading into a screened porch on the front of the house, but nobody appeared there and I went into a pose. Veronica began taking pictures from various angles and distances and was trying to balance herself on top of a fireplug in the street when I heard a rustling noise behind me. An elderly woman had come out on the porch, and as she opened the screen door a few inches I could see by her face that she was alarmed.

"What is it?" she asked in a quavering voice. "Are we losing it? Oh, please don't!"

"Pardon me, madam," I said, "but I was born in this house."

"Right out from under us!" she cried. "That's what you're going to do! I can tell! You don't need to try to fool me!"

"I was born right here in this house," I insisted, "and we just wanted to take some pictures, and I hope you don't mind."

She considered this explanation until she got it straight and then she brightened.

"Oh," she said. "Then you're not going to rent it right out from under us?"

That had been her first reaction, her greatest concern, because the housing shortage was just as acute in McLeansboro as elsewhere in the land, and if somebody rented a house out from under you, you were up the creek without a paddle.

I reassured her, and Veronica went on taking pictures and complaining about my inadequacy as a subject. She felt that I ought to look like an author instead of what I looked like; that there was little point in a picture of me the way I was. I told her that to look like an author I would have to stick a pipe in my face, or bush up my hair, or pose beside a fireplace with my hand on a large dog, or hanging in the rigging of a ship with a yachting cap on my head, or holding my chin in my hand with my forefinger laid up against my nose, or correcting galley proofs, or wearing a black beard. None of these poses appeared to fit the situation, so I just went ahead looking like the guy who had brought the laundry to the little house on Hancock Street.

When we had finished we hurried downtown to leave

the film and then went to Aunt Nellie's house. Aunt Nellie is a water-color artist of considerable talent, and over the years she has turned out hundreds of paintings. Many people have her do pictures of their homes, or of favorite scenes, and her standard fee for such commissions is a dollar and a half.

Being an artist myself, a literary artist, and a fervent admirer of money, I considered her pay per painting to be an outrage. I now wanted her to take the photographs of my birthplace when they were ready and execute a nice water color of it for me. I paid her what I thought she ought to be paid for the job, and when she protested I told her that I wanted an extra-special job done on my birthplace—no little old dollar-and-a-half thing. Since she had lived across the street from the house when I was born, she remembered it as it was then. In those days it set flat on the ground, whereas now it had been hoisted onto concrete blocks, and the front porch was a later addition, and the trees in the front yard were, of course, bigger than they were in 1906, and the electric meter fastened to the front wall of the house hadn't been there in my time. She'd rectify all these anachronisms in her painting and send it to me in New York as soon as she finished it.

That seemed to complete my mission in McLeansboro. John Stelle Day was coming up on the morrow, a Saturday. Whooping members of the American Legion already were pouring into town, and the dust in the air was so thick I was beginning to see mirages. The old fiddlers were tuning up, the National Barn Dance gang was on its way down from Chicago, John Stelle himself was arriving momentarily from Indianapolis, mules and plugs were being groomed for the races, and the bunting that flew for Truman and Churchill in Fulton was flying for Stelle in Egypt.

I suppose I should have stayed, but some urgent matters were awaiting me in St. Louis. Among other things, Lillian Friedman was telephoning, asking me to autograph books at Stix, Baer & Fuller on Saturday afternoon. She'd furnish us with the scarcest of all commodities—a suite in a hotel—if I'd do it. I didn't hesitate long.

Chapter 17

In the time of my innocence (up to and including the age of four) there was much talk in McLeansboro about St. Louis, not alone because it was the nearest metropolis but because the Louisiana Purchase Exposition, or World's Fair, had just been held there. Grandpa Caleb Smith had gone to the exposition, along with many other McLeansboroites, but he was the only local person to take along a bagful of bricks. During that period his plant was turning out thirty-five thousand bricks a day, which may or may not have been quite a few bricks. He entered his bricks at the fair and they took the prize for uniformity of color, wearing quality, and smoothness of surface. That's my grampaw. I never heard what prize they gave him—possibly a silver trowel or a pewter hod.

You see how Life is? You recognize how a thread of bricks runs through the history of my family? Remember the brick I threw at the old dame in Ohio? And there's deeper significance than that. Caleb Smith's bricks swept all before them in St. Louis. His grandson's books always go good in the same city, though not for uniformity of color, wearing quality, and smoothness of surface. I have never been in St. Louis except for brief periods, yet it is somehow in my nature to love the city. I love it because it has produced people I admire, such as Jack Alexander and Betty Grable and John Beggs (I admire them for different reasons). And I love it

because my books stay on the best-seller lists in St. Louis considerably longer than they do elsewhere, unless maybe Atlanta.

You likely know about Jack Alexander and Betty Grable. As for John Beggs, he was a man who made about forty million dollars by inventing the strap which straphangers cling to in subways and trolley cars. He was in the traction business and loved money, and he invented the strap because he figured it would help to crowd more people into his public conveyances, and he was right. I think perhaps that he was the champion penny pincher of all time. Even when he had all those millions he wouldn't eat a bite of lunch unless someone else paid for it; if nobody invited him out to lunch, he went hungry. He wore the same derby hat for twelve years. One day he went to the bank which helped him with his business affairs, and a vice-president of the bank accidentally sat down on the old derby hat and mashed it. John Beggs stomped out of the place and never again did a lick of business with that bank. In his home he refused to hire domestic help, but had stenographers who were employed by his several corporations come to his home after office hours and do all the chores. He compelled his office boy to shine his shoes daily, for free. The boy had some spunk and one day gave the old flatus an argument. He said he didn't mind contributing the labor involved in shining shoes but that the materials—the rags and brushes and polish—had to be paid for out of his own pocket and he felt that he ought to be reimbursed for it. Old Man Beggs had a quick answer for that. "Young man," he said, "I got mine by digging. I started digging when I was your age and I'm still digging. Right now I'm digging *you* for shines. You go and find someone to dig. That's the way it goes."

You see, the man had character, and a fine, admirable sort of American philosophy; he was a rugged individualist, epitomizing free enterprise and free shoeshines, and if I had been that office boy I'd have taken my heaviest brush and raised knots on his noggin.

Soon after reaching St. Louis, I was called in to a radio station and installed as a guest performer on one of those programs where people are told how to scallop a potato, how to do it with Duz, and why nursing mothers ought to drink a case of beer a day.

This radio program was conducted by an articulate young lady, and her guest performers used no scripts, everything being ad-lib. I mention it here because I made a small blunder during the broadcast and if any of my readers appear on similar programs they will be able to guard against the error I committed.

There are many people in this world who are able to "listen" to a long and boring conversation without ever hearing a word of it. These people may be found in groups where stories are being told. One man is telling a story. His listeners are simulating rapt attention, but they are not hearing a word of it; they are running over in their minds the story which *they* intend to tell when this colossal bore is finished with his. They have developed a technique of pretended listening—they nod, and they grin, and laugh, and occasionally they say "Uh-huh," and they do these things at the proper moments in the story being told, governing their faked reactions by the flow of sound without paying any attention to the actual words.

Now an ad-lib radio performance can be a rough experience for a person, such as myself, who is not a professional, not an actor. On this St. Louis program the glib young woman was talking a good part of the time, and while she galloped along I paid little or no attention to what she was saying, being quite busy searching my mind for clever remarks and sparkling anecdotes. At last we finished the thing and got off the air, and the young lady looked at me and started laughing.

"Did you hear what you said?" she wanted to know. "Back around the dog-food commercial?"

I couldn't seem to remember, so she had the engineer play the recording of the broadcast. Back around the dog-food commercial she had gone into an extensive discourse about me. During the actual broadcast I had not been listening to her at all; I had closed my mind against her words, remaining aware only of the ends of sentences, when I would murmur "Yes," or "Uh-huh," or "Ummmmm." There came a point now in the recording where she was saying:

". . . and I'm sure a great many of our listeners will agree that Mr. Smith is the foremost humorist in America today, that no one else has given us so much sheer joy as he has . . ."

Then, quite distinctly, came my own voice.

"That's right," I said.

For something over fifteen years I had been a regular reader of the Eldon *Advertiser,* a weekly newspaper published in my wife's home town, but I had never been to Eldon. Throughout those years, too, I had met scores of men and women and children from Eldon through the circumstance of their having called on us whenever they were in New York, and I spent long hours listening to the gossip about the people of the Missouri town.

Without ever having been within a hundred miles of it, I think I knew more about Eldon than I knew about any other town in the Midwest; certainly I was better acquainted with it than I was with McLeansboro. I knew who had babies or were going to have babies or couldn't have babies; I knew how the high-school basketball team was doing, and I not only knew the name of the substitute center on the team but could tell you the name of his girl friend and how they spent their time and what she wore when he took her to a party; if I had been snatched up suddenly and parachuted into the middle of Eldon and the urge came upon me to go to a movie, I very likely would have known what picture was playing at the Ozark Theater.

Of course when I finally got there it wasn't at all like I had visualized it. Much to my chagrin, it was better. Eldon is a town of approximately the size of McLeansboro, though it is not a county seat, and my wife and I have spent many years tossing sarcasms about birthplaces at each other. She had seen McLeansboro and now I saw Eldon, and in a moment of utter madness I remarked that her home town was nicer than mine; I'll never hear the end of it.

I had to go through another reception with punch, this time in a private home, and I didn't mind it much except for the chigger bites. Prior to the reception I had been invaded by chiggers—the first chiggers to get their teeth into me in thirty years or more, and apparently they found me juicy and palatable. Moreover, these Missouri chiggers had no sense of modesty and concentrated their attack in out-of-the-way places. When a person has chigger bites it is essential that he scratch them, and there were moments when I came close to flaunting all the rules of proper conduct and going at them with both hands. One thing kept me from it.

Back home we had a television set, which brought baseball and basketball and football and fights and track meets into our living room. I suppose the players on, say, a baseball team knew that they were being televised, but I think their consciousness of it faded at times and they forgot. A man, say, gets a two-base hit and then takes his lead off second. He moves around a bit and turns his head to locate the shortstop and second baseman. Sometimes the television camera stays on this base runner for a while, until action is resumed elsewhere. And sometimes the base runner decides to scratch himself, and he does it before they can get the camera off of him. This sort of thing happens in basketball, too, and occasionally in boxing, and quite often when a track meet is being televised. At my house it always evokes much laughter, and there is a neighbor lady who sometimes comes in of an afternoon and sits through an entire baseball game —not understanding anything whatever about it, but simply waiting to see a ballplayer scratch himself. In time, of course, this feature of television will disappear because wives of ballplayers will put a stop to it.

The reception in Eldon was characterized by extremes of decorum, everything being ordered and done by rule of Emily Post, and there were even some people who came down the reception line and bowed. I nearly went nuts. In such surroundings, among such polite people, I felt that I was worse off than a ballplayer with a television camera aimed at him, and I couldn't scratch. Had it been my arms, or my chest, or even my legs, I believe I could have done it. As it was, I had to wait until a lull came, at which point I'd scamper for the front porch and find a dark corner to do my scratching in. Even that procedure had its evil side, because after two or three trips to the porch I noticed some of the men eying me suspiciously, and it dawned on me that they thought I had a jug hidden outside; among most of the people in Eldon that would have been a greater social offense than scratching the chigger bites.

When we drove into Eldon we were greeted by my in-laws, including my wife's sister Hila, a New York City nurse who had gone home to care for her ailing father. Hila told me that there had been some excitement on the day before our arrival. She said that a young man wearing a wild look in his eyes came racing down the street on a bicycle, pulled in at the Simpson house, and began hammering on the front door.

When Hila opened the door he gasped out:

"Is that H. Bedford Smith here?"

"You mean H. Allen Smith?"

"That's him. Is he here? I wanna see him."

"No," said Hila, keeping her distance, "he's not here." She didn't like the looks of this guy at all. "Who are you, and what do you want to see him about?"

"I'm Stinky Purvis," he said. "That's what they call me, but they don't call me Stinky to my face, 'cause I kill 'em if they do."

"What do you want to see Mr. Smith about, Stinky?" asked my tactful sister-in-law.

"I'm gonna tell him off, that's what. I'm gonna tell him he didn't write them books. Not a one of them."

"Well," said Hila, "I'm sure he'd be glad to hear that. Who wrote them if he didn't write them?"

"His wife, that's who," said Stinky. "She wrote ever' one of them."

"I think you might be mistaken," said Hila. "Have you read the books?"

"No. I never read any of them, 'cause they're a fake. And I know who wrote 'em, all right. And I'm gonna tell him to his face. He ain't gettin' away with nothin' on me."

"What makes you think his wife wrote them?" Hila wanted to know.

"I don't *think* she wrote 'em. I *know* she wrote 'em. You remember when Mr. Smith was teachin' at the high school?"

"Yes," said Hila. Stinky had reference to another Mr. Smith, of which there are some even in Eldon.

"Well," said Stinky, "Mr. Smith told ever' one of them stories that's in them books—he told ever' one of 'em to your sister, and then she goes out and marries this other Smith, and she writes out all them stories she got in high school, and then *he* claims *he* wrote 'em. Nobody gets away with that kind of stuff around me, and I'll tell 'im so, right to his durn face."

Hila finally got rid of him, and didn't see him again after that. When she told me of his visit I said I thought I'd go seek him out and get his version of my great fraud at firsthand and speak sharply to him about it. I was going to do it, that is, until Hila gave me a physical description of him. He was a big, powerful guy, and once when they had put him in jail he had taken hold of the plumbing in his cell and pulled it out of the concrete floor, pipes and all. I considered this thing at some length and then decided that Hila's version of the story was certainly adequate; no use wasting valuable time just getting it repeated. Anyway, we learned that Stinky was not altogether available for an interview. Apparently he had gone from the Simpson house to the business district, where he started riding his bicycle at top speed on the sidewalks, zipping in and out between pedestrians; and when the town marshal sought to dissuade him from this sport, Stinky stood in defense of his constitutional rights and made as if to knock the marshal's head off. He was escorted to the town's little jail and locked up, and that same evening he set fire to the jail, but they got it put out before much damage was done.

We had a fine time in Eldon, especially during the hours of visiting with Vol Simpson, my wife's father. In the closing years of his life both his legs were amputated and replaced with artificial ones. He'd sit with one of them extended on a hassock and talk about it, rapping it sharply with a cane for punctuation.

"Best wood on earth's in that leg," he'd say, giving it a rap. "Came all the way from England—that wood. Better wood in 'er than's in Charlie McCarthy!"

In Eldon, I met the two women I always had wanted to see in the flesh. One of these was a town matron, member of a good family, meaning a family that always had money. A few years earlier she had been a devout movie fan and seldom missed a picture at the Ozark. She usually occupied a seat in the front row of the balcony, and one evening while she was comfortably settled there a flea bit her, and after that several fleas bit her. For the next couple of weeks every time she went to the movie the fleas ganged up on her, and finally she went to the proprietor, Tom Edwards, and lodged a complaint against them. Mr. Edwards, a progressive movie exhibitor, was shocked at this news. He began asking other patrons of his theater if any fleas had attacked them, and it soon developed that Mrs. X was the only customer upon whose person the insects enjoyed feeding. Nobody else was bothered by fleas—just Mrs. X. Mr. Edwards appreciated her patronage and he also realized that it would be bad for him if his theater got the reputation of having fleas in its balcony. So he closed down the place for a day and called in exterminators from St. Louis and they laid down a gas attack sufficiently powerful to annihilate a scourge of movie critics.

This operation was costly, of course, and when it was completed and the theater reopened Mr. Edwards wanted to know, understandably enough, if it had been a hundred-per-cent effective. There was only one way to find out. He called on Mrs. X and told her what had been done.

"Mrs. X," he said, "I've had this job done from one end of the house to the other, and tonight I'd like for you to come down and see if any more fleas bite you."

"Why me?" demanded Mrs. X a bit archly.

"Well," said Mr. Edwards, "the fleas never bothered anybody else. You were the only customer they ever bit, so how am I to——"

"Kindly get out of my house," said Mrs. X. Mr. Edwards got out, and thereafter Mrs. X stayed away from his theater. Mr. Edwards had made a tactical error, but Mrs. X now made a worse one. She talked about it, giving voice to her indignation all over town, and now everyone knows that fleas go for her.

I was also grateful for the opportunity of meeting the girl who ate the doily. This incident dates back quite a few years when the young lady in question was just blossoming into societyhood. Her mama had taught her good manners and poise and she knew enough not to use guest towels in the homes of her friends. Then she went to the fatal party. Along toward the end of this affair plates of ice cream were passed around and, in each case, the chunk of ice cream rested on a fancy paper doily, which in turn rested on the plate. Our young lady was likely very nervous and not thinking straight because she ate the ice cream *and* the doily. Like the story of Mrs. X and the fleas, this matter was bruited across Miller County. It has been more than twenty years since that party, and the benighted girl has become a wife and mother, but for purposes of identification she is still "The One, You Know, Who Ate the Doily." When she arrived at the Eldon reception she was no more than across the threshold when people began congregating around me and whispering excitedly, "Here she comes—the one, you know, who ate the doily." I suppose I could have asked her about it, but I didn't have the heart. Surely she must know that people describe her as the doily-eater, and certainly it must bother her at times. I felt a little sorry for her, as I've always felt a little sorry for Richard Knight, the lawyer, who once stood on his head at opening night of the Metropolitan Opera. All he did was stand on his head—just once, one time. The thing has pursued him relentlessly ever since. His name pops into the newspapers periodically, something to do with a divorce, or a journey, or a society party, or a court case. Always it is the same—the news item begins: "Richard Knight, the man who stood on his head at the Metropolitan Opera House, today was . . ." The poor guy can't go anywhere but that it follows him. He stops overnight, say, at a hotel in Tucson. The local newspapers report it: "Mr. Richard Knight, the man who stood on his head at the Metropolitan Opera, is a visitor in Tucson." It looks to me as if he'll never get away from it, and when he dies and his obituary is written, it will start out the same way. And his children and his grandchildren will inherit it, and many years from now his descendants will be described as having come down in an unbroken line from the man who stood on his head at the opera. The thing might even reach the point where the Metropolitan Opera will become known as "the institution where Richard Knight once stood on his head."

We drove south from Eldon to visit the Hollenbecks in Sikeston, Missouri, and I have little to report on that community except to say that it was powerful hot. I spent several hours drowsing in a chair in the hotel lobby, listening to a couple of drummers telling washroom stories. Disgusting. I wouldn't dream of repeating most of them here because they were vulgar, and anyway Bennett Cerf may already have used them. They were not really very funny, although

there was one that caused me, against my better judgment, to chuckle. One of the drummers said to the other:

"Now get this. There's a girl that loves a fella, loves him more than anything else in the world. She's gonna marry him any day and he loves her as much as she loves him. Now. There comes a time when that girl is entitled to spit right square in his face. If she didn't do it, then she wouldn't really love him. You tell me what circumstances would justify her in spitting right square in his face."

The second drummer didn't give up at once, but after a period of cogitation he was unable to come up with the answer, so he surrendered and wanted to know when that girl would be justified in spitting right square in the face of the man she loved.

Said the other: "When his mustache is on fire."

Driving around Sikeston with my brother-in-law-in-law (he being married to my sister-in-law), I noticed a large sign above the entrance to a sort of stockyard. It read:

SIKESTON BULL SERVICE

There was a large Army camp somewhere in the Sikeston area, and I learned that on week ends the soldiers came into town by the hundreds and headed for that sign. One by one they'd stand in front of it, strike a pose, and have their picture taken. What they did with the pictures is unknown to me, but thousands of them were taken, and sometimes on Saturday afternoons they'd be lined up for a block, awaiting their turn under the sign.

Chapter 18

On the homeward journey we passed through the same states we had crossed going west, but I have covered all incidents and observations worth recording—all save one. We stopped overnight in Columbus, Ohio, and early in the evening I was walking along one of the busy streets when I thought I saw, coming toward me, Theodore Roosevelt, twenty-fifth president of the United States. He was in the full regalia of the Rough Riders and he was striding along at a brisk clip. I stopped, and stared at him, and as he came closer and went past me, I saw that it was not Teddy Roosevelt; it was a man who looked a good deal like Teddy, and he did have on the authentic costume of the Roosevelt Rough Riders. I went over and leaned against a store front and considered the thing, and suddenly I realized that I was in the home town of James Thurber, that I shouldn't be alarmed at anything I might see—that it would not be too extraordinary if a Rough Rider leaped upon me and climbed up my back as if it were San Juan Hill and cried, "The dam has broke! Go east!" Subsequently I learned that Spanish-American War veterans were having a convention in town.

Back on my own private hill in Westchester, I sat for a long time and thought about the adventure just finished. Going over it incident by incident, there seemed to be no sadness connected with it; I was no longer disturbed by the fact that an entire year had been removed from my life span or by the discovery that I wasn't who I was. I finally got a copy of the *Illinois Guide,* and it had no McLeansboro in it. I remembered how I couldn't get a shave in Defiance; how a goat lay chewing a cud amid the ruins of Idle Hour at Huntington; how Spike Jones ruined my moment-of-glory in an Indianapolis department store; how John Stelle Day deprived me of a hotel room in the town of my birth; the hiccups of the man with the roto-rooter.

Before long a package came in the mail, and it was Aunt Nellie's water color of the house where I was born. It was a beautiful job, and I thought perhaps I'd talk my publisher into using it as a frontispiece for this book. I planned on having a nice frame put around it and picked out the place on the wall of my study where I would hang it.

Then my mother came to visit me, and I got out the painting, eager for her to see the reverence in which I held the house where she bore me.

She looked at it and said:

"Why, son, *that's* not the house you were born in. You were born in a little cottage a couple of blocks from this place. I ought to know."

Now at last a darkling cloud came over me, and a great sadness took me in its grip; but only for a moment. I said a bad word, a word containing more than three letters and less than five, and preceded by "Oh." I said it right in front of my own mother, and she didn't speak a word in protest. I think maybe she understood.

LOW MAN on a TOTEM POLE

H. Allen Smith's first laugh classic. The hero, a prize fighter who wrote love stories. "Youse gotta read it, it will fill ya with passion."

BY H. ALLEN SMITH

Of H. Allen Smith, Fred Allen said, when introducing his first book LOW MAN ON A TOTEM POLE: "Mr. Smith is the screwball's Boswell . . . by choice he is a biographer to the dispensable man. The world is his laboratory, the human race his clinic."

NEW YORK HERALD TRIBUNE

"When it comes to egging people on and serving up the omelette, he is an artist."

NEW YORK TIMES

"Very nearly as lighthearted as the Pickwick papers . . . One thing about Mr. Smith is that he is not in the least bored. He writes with an unself-conscious, unforced brightness. . . . LOW MAN ON A TOTEM POLE *is funny.*"

LIFE IN A PUTTY KNIFE FACTORY

More of Smith's Leprechaun Humor, with Characters from the Wack's Museum——

The minister who was a whiz at burnball . . .
The Bust Pocket maker whose passion was postage stamps . . .
Mr. Ramshaw, an inconsiderate eagle . . .
The Strip Tease Picket who had a way with mules . . .
and many more crazy characters . . .

The critics say:

"Jam packed with a thousand dollars' worth of laughs."—CHICAGO SUN

"Better than his TOTEM POLE tome."—WALTER WINCHELL

"Smith has the touch of a slightly drunken elf swinging from the chandeliers . . . but on him it looks good."—CHICAGO DAILY NEWS

"H. Allen Smith's book is a twentieth-century wonderland. He is a screwball with a style and stiletto and his life and time contain as many wacky vignettes as a Dali movie."—DOROTHY HILLYER in the BOSTON HERALD

by
H. ALLEN SMITH

H. ALLEN SMITH

Lost in the Horse Latitudes

The author as seen by his friends . . .

"About the funniest writing man in New York is H. Allen Smith."—CHARLES B. DRISCOLL

"A live-wire newspaper interviewer gives off shocking sparks."—JIMMIE FIDLER

"Required reading . . . rich human stuff loaded with laughs."—DAMON RUNYON

"Read *Low Man on a Totem Pole* three times in one year . . . have had *Lost in the Horse Latitudes* less than a week and have read it twice. That's the kind of Smith fan I am."—AL JOLSON

THIS IS RHUBARB

WACKY RIBALD CHEERFUL

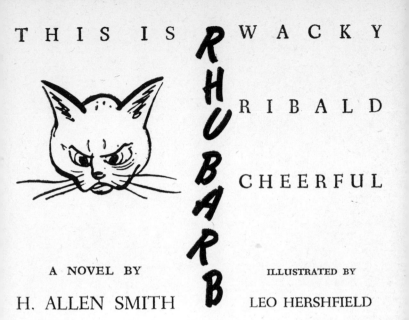

A NOVEL BY

H. ALLEN SMITH

ILLUSTRATED BY

LEO HERSHFIELD

H. Allen Smith's laugh riot. About a cat who inherited a baseball team and a million bucks, who loves tennis balls and hates dogs.

DESERT ISLAND DECAMERON

An anthology of humorous pieces by such writers as Robert Benchley, Ring Lardner, Mark Twain, with an introduction to the book and to each selection by

H. ALLEN SMITH

"Will certainly lighten many a weary hour during the months to come. Original and genuinely funny, it will take a dour man to keep a straight face beyond page three, which is where the text begins."— NEW YORK POST

"H. Allen Smith is headed for one of the rare niches reserved for America's top humorists."—CHICAGO SUN

"A humor book calculated to make your wrinkles the happy kind."—PHILADELPHIA RECORD